Why Do Men Have Nipples?

Vicar Michael

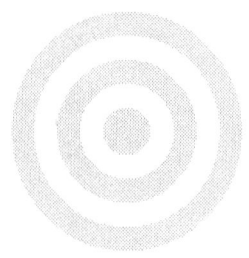

authorHOUSE®

AuthorHouse™ UK Ltd.
500 Avebury Boulevard
Central Milton Keynes, MK9 2BE
www.authorhouse.co.uk
Phone: 08001974150

First published by AuthorHouse 8/21/2007

ISBN: 978-1-4343-1610-3 (sc)

Printed in the United States of America
Bloomington, Indiana

This book is printed on acid-free paper.

Table of Contents

Introduction

Facts and Questions

They serve no purpose - So why do men have nipples?

Men have nipples because all human embryos begin life female.

Black Brown White Yellow delusions serve to disprove each other -

Electro Magnetism (EM) forms carbon based life

Time and Space are Infinite

Universe is Infinite - It is not a house with walls floors and a roof

I kill carrots - I eat carrots - I hate carrots

Love is a gift - Achieve I love me to achieve I love you

Love is spelt L O V E - Live is spelt L I V E - Similar - Association

Evil is L I V E backwards E V I L.

Hate is spelt H A T E - Ate is spelt A T E - Similar - Association

Do you want everyone to love you or do you want everyone to hate you?

The word god creates racism, sexism and conflict -

Black, brown, white, yellow - Male or Female - Arguments begin - War

The word g - o - d is based on the word good.

Electro Magnetism can be good and bad.

The Sun creates life and can also give you skin cancer - Bad

The Sun is part of the Electro Magnetic energy in the Universe.

The Sun has the potential for Love and Hate.

Humans can choose - Continue life on Earth or end.

Do you want everyone to love you or do you want everyone to hate you?

The word devil is based on the word evil.

Electro Magnetism is good and evil.

Some would call it Ying Yang or balance.

The Sun is in balance.

The Sun is a chemical reaction in dynamic equilibrium.

The Sun does not get any warmer or any cooler.

If the Universe is a laboratory - Who is the scientist?

All living matter in the Universe using telekinesis is the scientist.

Humans hate vegetables - We kill them - We eat them.

Humans can love all animals by not killing or eating them.

Humans can then achieve balance or Ying Yang.

All living matter is part of one infinite computer controlling chemical reactions.

All living matter is god and the devil combined as one.

The god or good in us makes us do good things and hopefully we can love all animals.

The devil or evil in us makes us kill vegetables - Appendix Organ?

Do you want everyone to love you or do you want everyone to hate you?

The question above is for animals including the human one.

Do we need to kill vegetables or could we live on minerals produced naturally - Water House

The scientist in all of us will tell us when the time is right for Water House.

Is Water House actually our way off Planet Earth if Earth was to fail or we needed to leave?

Is Water House a Flying Saucer?

When you say god or spirit do you mean Electro Magnetism?

Chapter 1

Teaching 1

Good morning global family.

I love everyone in our global family equally.

Turn to the person on the right and tell them "I love you".

Turn to the person on your left and tell them "I love you".

Now say I love everyone in the global family equally.

I have started this teaching in this church and you will notice I have had all images of violence, death and destruction removed from this church.

I simply could not teach love with those types of images around me.

After all vicars like me have been teaching love for many years and it would be hatred to nail us vicars to crosses.

Glorifying killing is illegal in the UK.

The message is we vicars teach love and not killing.

The teaching each week will concentrate on love to begin with.

By love we mean not killing living creatures.

So why is there a picture of an appendix behind me?

The appendix is our love of animals organ in our bodies.

We have an appendix to remove the green part of vegetable matter called chlorophyll.

Eating animals is equivalent to having a miniature blood transfusion with the wrong blood group.

Would a doctor advise a blood transfusion with the wrong blood group?

Poisoning the body - Health problems? Senile dementia?

A Doctor said milk is for cows.

The appendix organ was used many years ago when we lived on green matter and probably exclusively.

We can live as vegans without the appendix working for us.

So this organ is proof that like many other animals with an appendix that we evolved not needing to kill and eat animals.

Electro Magnetism (EM) has designed us to be vegans.

Horses and many others have an appendix and have been successfully and healthily fuelling their bodies with vegetable matter.

So the appendix is our love organ.

We love many animals and do not kill and eat them.

We worry about their environment and general welfare.

It is strange that we would never kill and eat a swan but some people eat other birds.

However if you ask most people if they could kill an animal.

Most say they could not.

This is because our appendix is telling us that we do not need to kill and eat animals.

Imagine a world where humans did not kill any animals including the human animal.

The outcome would be peace.

The appendix is our love organ.

So all my teachings will begin with love for our global family followed by the latest scientific knowledge.

In the past the church has been slow to move forward and has resisted new knowledge.

The children have learnt new knowledge at school and it has made the church seem old fashioned and in some cases appearing untruthful based upon common knowledge.

For example we used to talk about the hands of something they called god watering the seeds.

A child would go to school and learn that the sun heated the water in the sea causing the water to evaporate rise and create clouds.

These clouds are then blown above the land meet cold air and precipitation occurs commonly called rain.

The children having learnt the new knowledge at school taught by teachers with expert knowledge and qualifications then question the churches somewhat odd ideas compared with their modern knowledge taught at school.

The children then think the vicar is lacking in knowledge and the vicar loses credibility.

The child decides not to go to church anymore.

This is sad because the church teaches love and the child loses this valuable teaching because the church has not decided to move with the times.

We hear many stories these day of teachers struggling with noisy badly behaved children.

Is this happening because the child is not getting the love message from the church?

Could it also be that the church could be telling the older people to tell the children not to believe new knowledge in the school because the church has felt threatened by new knowledge and maybe the church has become too proud to change.

Some of its old ideas are no longer believable as new scientific facts have become available.

What I as a vicar now want to do is to keep teaching the love message which is good and has been taught by the church for many years and add up to date knowledge based on scientific fact.

I will talk about things, which have been scientifically proven and truthful as opposed to guesswork and theories.

Did an asexual creature give birth to twins, male and female or did a hermaphrodite give birth to creatures of both sexes while we were evolving in water?

Now I am guilty of speculating, interesting though.

What we do know is that all living creatures are made of particles and electricity.

We know that particles fuse with other particles to create chemicals.

All living things have chromosomes in their cells. In the human case when a female egg fuses with a sperm from the male the 23 pairs of chromosomes line up and fuse with the use of electro magnetism (EM).

Electronic information is transferred and details like the colour of eyes and the complete instructions for making the human being are present in the chromosomes.

If the human is male the human has the XY chromosomes.

If the human is female it is usually XX.

Recent scientific research has shown that an embryo was born as a female but had the male XY chromosomes configuration and should in normal conditions have become male.

The scientific research showed that because the testosterone hormone which is responsible for creating the male gender manufactured by instructions on the Y chromosome had not been produced the human embryo was born female.

If you look at the male penis at the very end what does it remind you of?

It is a miniature clitoris. So the clitoris come first and converts into a penis in the case of the male. The penis does not shrivel and turn into a clitoris.

The testicles begin life in the ovary positions before dropping. So then does ovary matter convert into testicle matter when the hormone testosterone is present? No testosterone and the embryo remains female.

The default for human embryo is female as is proven by the XY lady described above in scientific research.

I feel sure the scientist will one day be able to show us how particles and electricity fused together and what electro magnetic forces were present to form the living creatures we are today.

For example we know that the moon is kept in its orbit by electro magnetic forces.

The moon is made of particles and electricity and so is Planet Earth, as we know.

You may have heard of the North and South Pole.

So the Earth is a large magnet and so is the moon.

In physics you may have moved one magnet with another by the north pole pushing the north pole or the south pole pushing the south pole.

Alternatively the north pole can attract the other magnet's south pole.

Everything including us humans are magnetically attracted to Planet Earth.

Our brains have to calculate magnetic attraction in order that we can stand up and move.

What we do know is that the electro magnetic effect could affect the fusing of particles which make up the chromosomes in living things.

We know for example that the moon is responsible for the tides magnetically attracting the water or repelling the water.

Can character traits be dictated by the movement of the planets and stars which cause an electro magnetic stirring effect?

The moon is also thought to be responsible for the menstrual cycle.

The menstrual cycle operates by the production of female hormones.

Chemical reactions require energy.

The moon's electrical energy is in some way involved with the creation of the hormones.

As I mentioned at the beginning we should be one loving global family.

We should love each other equally regardless of whether our chromosome instructions are close to someone else's or more distant.

Some people decide to get married.

They say that 50% get divorced.

My chromosome providers are divorced.

So why does marriage appear to be failing for 50%?

I believe having been married myself that we as humans get bored.

It is not that we do not love one another.

We do not want to kill and put the other person in the oven and eat them.

Unfortunately the sex seems to go off.

People start having regular sex but this in many cases slows down and becomes less regular.

Sometimes to the point where it completely stops.

This leads to sexual frustration.

It is thought that men in particular have a desire to spread their seed around.

Marriage attempts to stop this normal behaviour.

This leads to sexual frustration, which is passive anger, which can lead to war.

Arranged marriages where people are forced to be together could also lead to problems as the two people possibly do not find each other sexually attractive.

They love one another in a global family sense but possibly do not find each other sexually attractive.

If a man forces himself on a woman without the women saying yes to sex this is usually referred to as rape and is quite wrong.

I also feel that prostitution is wrong.

The woman possibly does not want to have sex with a man but still has sex even though she might not want to have sex.

I would also call this rape.

My vision of the future is that everyone should have their own individual home.

This goes for young people as well who will get their independence early.

They will be loved and cared for by the global family and the church and school will teach them love, good moral conduct and up to date knowledge.

Some people may wish to live together for a period of time.

The good news is that everyone has a place to live and those people can live in their own individual homes.

Traditional marriages cause many problems when people decide to split.

The house has to be sold causing much stress.

In some cases people remain living together and are unhappy.

They have a mortgage and possibly financial problems.

They cannot afford to split up and live together unhappily.

Sexual frustration occurs as neither is interested in the other person.

This is a sad unsatisfactory situation which can lead to people being on anti-depressants.

The new way of living is designed to give everyone freedom.

No one owns anyone else.

I believe it will create happiness.

If we look at suicide bombers they are told they will meet 20 virgins if they blow both themselves and other people up.

It appears then that this is their fantasy.

This would lead me to believe that they are sexually frustrated.

This may be more likely with arranged marriage.

I am convinced that if people were busy having sex they would be happier and would not want to blow themselves up causing destruction and distress.

Marriage - Sexual Frustration - Passive Anger - War.

I believe as mentioned earlier we can live as vegans and should.

It says I am in touch with my appendix my love organ.

There are also many health benefits through going on this diet.

For example I am a vegan and my cholesterol level is below 3.

I know some people who eat dairy and egg products and animals and have a cholesterol level over 6.

So eating dairy and eggs can cause problems.

As mentioned previously if people had to kill the animal before they ate it many could not.

This is because we have the appendix and we know we do not need to kill animals.

There are now many products available including chocolate ice cream made with Soya milk although it is the love of animals that should influence our decision.

I do not agree with capitalism, as I believe in love.

Many continue to kill and eat animals because of the animal killing industry, which is in total conflict with what our appendix is telling us.

Some people eat sheep but do not want to think that they are eating a lamb.

How many could kill a lamb?

The truth is we hate everything we eat.

We kill it.

We do not love the food we eat.

It does not die for us.

We kill it.

We hate it.

Capitalism causes many problems.

If we all went vegan it would cause problems and people's jobs would be affected.

We need a serious rethink on capitalism.

I would prefer to see it end and introduce an interactive democracy using modern communications, which would represent the individual.

The current system of politicians ends up being sponsored by people who wish to further their interests by influencing government.

This leads to a democracy, which is not impartial.

The other negative about the current system of politicians is that many people are travelling long distances everyday causing environmental problems.

In addition if they don't travel back to the area where they were elected they cannot properly represent people.

We have poverty and environmental problems all of which could be solved.

Because people are not keen on paying in the current capitalist system the action is limited.

Many continue to starve to death.

These people are part of our global family.

We do not want to kill and eat them.

We love them.

So let us sort this problem out immediately.

Many saw the Live 8 concert and many were shocked at what has been going on for many years.

Governments tell the people taxes will have to rise and people decide not to take action even though their appendix love organ is saying this is wrong.

I wear the **MAKE**POVERTY**HISTORY** band.

The oil industry is important to the current capitalist system.

There are many people employed.

We need to take action to reduce carbon emissions.

The trouble is if we take action this will affect the world's biggest industry.

Electricity can be sourced by introducing a thermal coupling device into water.

The heat energy is converted to electrical energy.

Add a borehole to source warm water and we have no energy problems.

Money is the root of all evil.

Take money out of the equation and our problems can be sorted.

Some people on the instruction from a hallucination have invaded areas of the world causing imbalance in the world.

To many it appears they are trying to control oil reserves, as they are worried about running out of oil which will run out one day in any case.

I believe we have the technology but industry stifles innovation to preserve existing jobs, which if you think about it in a capitalist economy is the thing to do.

Take money out of the equation and I believe new technology would be implemented to the benefit of Planet Earth.

If we don't take action I believe there will be more unrest in the world which could lead to more wars which could destroy Planet Earth.

Is this what we want?

If we take the right action now and end the current capitalist system the struggle for oil will stop and the wars will not happen.

The choice is ours.

To do nothing is suicide and murder leaving our beautiful planet damaged and possibly sending it into hibernation for many years.

Is this what we want?

If children work hard at school then they will get their desired job.

They will still compete to be top of the class.

The difference is everyone will have a decent life with people working half the hours some do under capitalism and no pointless jobs like insurance and banking that don't serve any purpose producing nothing.

People will have the Freedom they have always wanted for themselves, future generations and forever.

The hallucinations that people see in their minds are not real although they appear to be.

Remember they never get any older.

There are black, brown, white and yellow skinned hallucinations.

According to Peter at Wokingham Mental Health in Reading UK Jesus is shown as a different colour dependent upon where you live.

I would have thought people would have thought of this as suspicious.

A doctor has told me that these are symptoms of schizophrenia and indeed I have suffered from schizophrenia and have seen the white hallucination, which appeared real to me at the time.

On consulting with a doctor he confirmed that they are not real.

These hallucinations seem to have been controlling people's lives and in many cases their instructions have lead to terrible loss of life and suffering.

They are supposed to have been good it appears their instructions are bad.

If you see these hallucinations it is best to ignore them and consult with a psychiatric doctor.

The brain is made of particles and electricity and acts as a computer.

Just like a computer it can send and receive messages, similar to sending an E-mail and making a mobile phone call.

The particles in the Universe carry the signal electronically.

Some are conscious of this and some are not.

There is a society who call themselves masons although this is an untruth as most of them do not work with stone.

The name masons is used to hide the truth which is something they are supposed to believe in.

They have conscious telepathic and telekinetic powers.

They categorise people - Faithful - Paul McCartney - Freemason.

The Faithful are not conscious of telepathy, hearing thoughts and other psychic powers and do not have a death threat suicide pact.

They can be manipulated by those with conscious psychic powers.

Paul McCartney has telepathic powers but does not have an oath.

Those who call themselves Freemasons do because it is a false name to cover up for what they can do in the psychic world.

They have a psychiatric problem as they agree an oath which is a suicide pact which is both insane and illegal under current law.

The doctors and police do nothing and therefore one can only conclude that they are protecting this society and may have agreed the suicide pact along with many others.

They are in the majority and therefore think they can't be wrong until now when some have finally made them see sense.

They are supposed to believe in love, truth and relief.

In reality they threaten to kill their membership.

Why Do Men Have Nipples?

How strange and both insane and illegal.

Maybe they should ask themselves "Is it insane to swear an oath that could lead to suicide?"

They say it is symbolic.

It is symbolic.

It is symbolic of murder.

They say they would die for one another.

I wonder how many would shoot themselves through the brain if another member needed their heart?

How many have agreed to have their organs donated on recycling?

Just how is having your tongue cut out, throat cut, heart ripped out and disembowelment going to save someone's life?

It is truly a mental illness and it needs curing.

I get the feeling they started out with good intentions.

Something went wrong and they have evolved into a mind control society with death threats and secrets which completely conflict with the original ideas of love, truth and relief.

Thousands dying of starvation everyday.

So where is the relief?

If they believe in love then why do we have
capitalism which is a hateful system?

If anyone asks you if you want to join the masons
simply say you do not work with stone and refuse.

If they push, go on to say that the lodge's suicide
pacts are both insane and illegal under current law.

They also think they were made by various black,
brown, white and yellow gods.

As we know this is absolute nonsense and
they are hallucinating which is symptomatic of
schizophrenia.

It is mental illness and needs sorting.

Are people with so called mental illnesses simply
the victims of electro magnetic hypnotism like
guided robots doing strange things as they are
being controlled by lodge members?

How sad that many are locked up for year upon
year because they disagree with the lodges.

They are drugged up to stop their brains from
functioning.

The lodges see these poor people as a threat and
they are punished mentally.

It appears the lodges do not like people to say the
words "I love you" to everybody.

How sad.

They say mental illness is caused by chemical changes in the brain.

As we know all chemical reactions require energy.

Could it be the lodges use joint kinetic energy to change the chemicals in people's brains and they begin hallucinating gas or visual hallucinations planted in their brains by the virtual graphics studio run by the lodges?

Lodge members appear to be both insecure and aggressive.

They monitor thoughts and if they do not like what you are thinking you may shout out as your body's electro magnetic system can be controlled by lodge members by REMOTE CONTROL as you would control a TV.

They also grip the hand in strange ways sometimes crushing fingers to promote their strange handshake.

This is all done electronically as we know the body is made of particles which are infinitely small and electricity.

Anything creating an electronic signal can be tuned into and that includes TVs, Radios, people's ears, eyes and all their senses.

If you think about it eyes are cameras and ears are microphones.

The brain can be electronically calibrated to achieve these extra functions.

This is what the lodges do to lodge members - They calibrate minds.

So most are not masons they are a telepathic society.

The sky is blue because the particles in the atmosphere refract the light forming the blue colour.

Plants grow through a process called photosynthesis, which uses the sun's light to break water in the plant into hydrogen and oxygen.

The plant then gives out oxygen, which we animals breathe.

The hydrogen is then combined with the carbon dioxide we breathe out making carbohydrates for the plant.

The plant then fuses nitrogen with the carbohydrate to form proteins to help the plant grow.

The really good news is that a scientist Newton said Matter can neither be created nor destroyed.

We are made of matter and electricity therefore we cannot be destroyed.

So we will live forever in the Universe.

Heaven and Hell are the Universe.

Recycling the possibilities are endless.

Particles can exist as part of a liquid solid or gas.

Water is actually two gasses combined together.

If you told someone this 1500 years ago they would probably have said you were mad.

Sometimes people don't like change.

They feel uncomfortable with the ramifications of the new knowledge.

Perhaps some who command respect feel they may lose respect if they are seen to be wrong.

As a consequence the church has fought off new ideas.

Newton's law confirmed everlasting life.

The church put Einstein under pressure to try to disprove Newton as Newton was saying there was no beginning and that matter had been in the Universe forever.

The church got upset.

Einstein went down with schizophrenia during his attempt to disprove Newton.

If you take an apple and keep halving it will not disappear.

You just keep using a stronger microscope.

Nothing cannot become something.

Something has been here forever.

Newton is correct and yes we will live forever.

Killing Jesus was the worst thing we have ever done.

This is the reason I have asked the church to remove all crosses and any other images of death and destruction.

Imagine if Jesus had not been killed there would have been thousands of vicars teaching love and the world would have become a loving caring place hundreds of years ago with no wars, and no famine and no environmental problems today.

Jesus was killed and look at the problems we now have.

It was wrong to kill Jesus.

If someone was nailed to a cross and murdered today the police would arrest the people who did it and they would be charged with murder.

It is illegal.

Jesus was the first vicar.

Jesus taught the vicars to teach love and say to the congregation to love one another.

So are we saying all vicars should be nailed to a cross?

Why Do Men Have Nipples?

Vicars teach love and now up to date science
and not guess work and theories which children
disprove when they go to school.

We want those children and people back in church
to get the love message and fantastic scientific
truth which enlightens people and gives them a
better informed life and in many cases makes
people happy.

Remember due to Newton we will live forever not
Jesus.

Killing Jesus achieved nothing.

It was very sad and probably the worst thing we
have ever done.

John Nash the famous mathematician believes the
Universe is infinite.

The thought that some people have that the
Universe has walls, floor and a roof seems to be
based on the fact that we live in houses with walls,
floor and a roof.

The Universe does not have walls, floor and a roof
and no one has seen any sign posts saying second
Universe.

Therefore I agree with John Nash who was also
given a bad time going down with schizophrenia
probably because he was challenging old ideas.

A few years later he wins the Noble Prize.

What more can I say?

Don't fight science.

It provides us with the truth.

I feel sure that people who say survival of the fittest are pleased we have hospitals.

What would some do without their spectacles or contact lenses?

Thou shalt not kill should be replaced with the phrase we should reduce the number of species we kill.

We were designed with an appendix.

We know we do not need to kill and eat animals.

Actions speak louder than words.

Love - Reduce killing - No death threats.

Truth - No secrets.

Relief - Everyone fed and housed.

Love thy neighbour.

You love me.

Chapter 2

Messages to Yoko

Talking about COME TOGETHER did John mean
the lodge members and faithful coming together
as one partnership? Those who call themselves
masons are not telling the truth as most have been
trained to do a job and do not work with stone.
John knew about the subliminal thought world
No. 9 Dream "River of sound" "More I cannot say"
"What more can I say". He wanted to tell the truth
but something was stopping him from telling the
whole truth. That I believe is my role. To tell what
John wanted to. The human psyche is about to be
turned upside down. Come together as telepathic
partnership - Is that what John would want? Please
find my paper below. Love thy neighbour Michael

We have a factory manufacturing WMDs just down
the road from me. Strange how it is OK for us to
produce them. Love thy neighbour Michael

Hi there lovers
Everything is made of atoms and electrons.
A bit like an electronic "soup" (Vegan one of
course!) throughout the universe which I believe
is INFINITE. Are we causing the soup to become
"stirred up" by abusing our planet through burning
fossil fuels and is this the reason for "electronic"
hurricanes? I could be wrong. We feel for anyone
who has suffered as a result of a natural disaster.
Are disasters natural or are we causing the

problems through our abuse of the planet. Love Michael.

Money is the root of all evil. I suggest we have a FREE vote to Abolish Money. If we live in a Free Democratic World we should have the right to a vote on money. Or do we have fascism run by the lodges? Love thy neighbour Michael

I believe John's electrons were absorbed into the Universe's electron store when he died and now occupy a new body or bodies somewhere in the Universe. If time and space are infinite then so is life. Einstein said you cannot make or destroy matter. John's atoms (mainly hydrogen, oxygen and carbon) would naturally be recycled. You eat a potato. You breathe out carbon dioxide. The potato plant takes in the carbon dioxide and the potato grows and so on. Love Michael.

They probably hallucinate various gods. Strange how they never get any older. Under their logic it should look life a dinosaur as these were around millions of years before human beings. What about Neanderthal man? What did their god look like then? It is a con and most of us have fallen for it including me until I saw the light and consulted my education. The world is suffering from a mental illness. Does anyone die for anyone or are they murdered. What does Yoko think?

Is Yoko a VEGAN? Love Michael.

Marriage = Sexual Frustration = Passive Anger = War. Love thy neighbour Michael

John would not have been popular with the arms industry. Peace is bad for business. Would the US

economy collapse if there was peace in the world?
About time those who are supposed to believe
in Love Truth and Relief thought Love Truth and
Relief and did Love Truth and Relief. Just who
is controlling the US government? The DaVinci
Code? Who controls money in the US? Who does
the pyramid or single eye represent? Suggestion
- Continue the Love revolution by finishing your
letters and E-mails with the words Love thy
neighbour and avoid Times Roman Font. Ban the
cross - Erect the heart. Love thy neighbour Michael

Peace or arms industry? Love thy neighbour
Michael

When you say g-d do you mean electro
magnetism? Love thy neighbour Michael

Was JFK soft on communism? What happened to
him? Did John have communist tendencies? What
happened to him? Was Mark Chapman a robot
with someone holding a remote control? Telepathic
hypnotism? Let us forget the past. Many have
made mistakes. Do we need politicians when
we have many ways to communicate? Leaders
cause problems whether they are capitalist or
communist. Could we have a proper interactive
democracy using phone, mobile cell and E-mail?
Could we call it VotePOINT? The first suggestion to
go on VotePOINT could be: 1. Should we abolish
money? Let the people decide. Love thy neighbour
Michael

Good Friday? Should read Bad Friday. No one
benefited from the killing of Jesus. It is about
time this sick idea came to an end. We should all
love one another and not use the killing of Jesus
as some sort of sin sponge. The church sends

out mixed messages. Love one another but if you cannot don't worry Jesus was killed for you. This is truly sick. A mental illness. Electro magnetism is the Creator and Destroyer. 500 million years ago there were no humans on planet Earth. Only dinosaurs. Do they still believe in a human god? It is a hallucination. The people have been brainwashed and are now suffering from a mental illness. Am I supposed to reject the scientific knowledge taught to me by my biology teacher? We simply have to learn to love one another. Oil will run out. If we keep going down the Greed Road we will end up with nuclear war. We need to reject capitalism. Money is the root of all evil. We must learn to love one another and not threaten each other with a stupid suicide pact or worthlessness. We should have no secrets. If people genuinely believe in Love, Truth and Relief then it is about time we showed it with our actions. Suicide pacts and threats of worthlessness are NOT love. If we believe in the truth then don't have secrets. Become transparent. I have nothing to hide. I have had my testicles surgically dropped. When I wipe my bottom I spit on the tissue paper as your saliva is a good antiseptic. I have no secrets. This is the way I am to remain. Secrets create insecurity. Love Michael.

Go vegan. Then no human will kill any animal. Actions speak louder than words. PEACE. Love thy neighbour Michael

Hi Dave
Some people told me the AIDS virus was man made. Are they true?
Love Michael.

Hi there lovers
Well done to Yoko for the advert in the Sunday
Times in the UK. Do you want a laugh? Log on
to "http://www.katebush.com" . If it makes you
laugh log on to "http://www.telepathicpartnership.
com" If it does not make you laugh you better
go and suffer down the masonic lodge with the
other idiots. Come on you know it is stupid. If you
really want to suffer and die we will take you to a
desert and leave you with no food and water. You
do not seriously want to do that do you? Leave
the masons. Join us. We believe in LOVE, TRUTH
and RELIEF and ELECTRO MAGNETISM. Sounds
familiar. I am a vegan. We don't just say it we do
it. Talk the talk. Walk the walk. We do not threaten
to kill anyone. Love Michael.

Men should understand that the truth from a
scientific study on sexuality done in the US is that
the reason men have nipples is because all human
embryos begin female to the point where there
is a lady in the US who is XY chromosome make
up and should therefore be male but because
the testosterone did not kick in the embryo was
delivered female. So much for Adam and Eve.
It should therefore be Eve and Adam. Millions
of days. Electro Magnetism. Infinity. Ever get
the feeling we have been fed masculine rubbish
brain wash for years? Come on Sari. Let us have
freedom of speech. Love thy neighbour Michael

Jesus was murdered. He did not die for anyone.
Love Michael.

Do we forgive ourselves for letting 20000 people
die of starvation every day or should we do
something about it? Love Michael.

Are human beings programmed to kill? By who? Why have human got an appendix? We were herbivores. Therefore we should not kill animals. So why did we change? Who made us change? Love Michael.

Penis or vagina? ELECTRO MAGNETISM is the creator. TIME and SPACE are INFINITE. Love Michael.

Absolutely. Black god white god? - ELECTRO MAGNETISM. Love Michael

Who tells people to commit suicide? Is it suicide or telepathic murder? Love Michael.

Build on agreements. Adam and Eve took how many days for the creator to make? One day or several million. Men have nipples which suggest Eve came first. All human embryos begin life female. What colour was Eve? Black as apparently we came out of the Congo in Africa. The word god should be deleted. Everything is made of Atoms and Electrons. Electro magetism can do good things and bad things. The Sun makes plants grow which gives us oxygen. Too much Sun and we get skin cancer which could kill us. The word Force is more appropriate. What do you all think? Love Michael.

Killing Jesus saved no one from anything. There is nothing to be saved from except the imagination of human beings. Heaven and hell are here on Earth. GET REAL. About time those fmasons gave god a shave in their graphics studio. Imagination. The biggest lie ever told is the idea of a god. Electro Magnetism is REAL. Sun, Moon and every atom pushing pulling fusing. What do you all think? Love Michael

People do not want to talk about it. The telepathic fmasons control the world and the way we think through telepathic brainwashing. I love the fmasons- Just don't understand what they are trying to achieve as 20000 die of starvation today. Relief Love Truth? Love Michael

Why do people hate one another? Hatred comes from within. The fmasons are behind a cruel ritual which leaves the person valueless. The person then hates themselves. They then have the gift of hate. Human greed. Money. What makes some people good and others killers? Go VEGAN. They care. Love Michael.

Time for logic and love and not fairy stories and hypocrisy. Love thy neighbour Michael

Hi there lovers
Why have different sexes? The reason men have nipples is because all human embryos begin life female. We are all creatures of the Universe. Did you know we are all made of atoms and electrons and this is the reason we are telepathic? John's song # 9 Dream. The freemasons are aware of telepathic communication and so are Paul McCartneys. The faithful are not aware of telepathy although we are all doing it all the time. The freemasons threaten to kill each other. Paul McCartneys do not. Are Paul and Yoko friends now? I hope so. We should all love one another. One family not millions of them. Love Michael.

Hi there lovers
All human embryos begin life FEMALE. This is the

reason men have nipples. As a child my testicles did not drop. They were in the ovary position. So do testicles start life as ovaries? Look carefully at the male part and compare the end of the male part (Very end) and compare it with the female part. Look sort of similar. What do you think? Ha Ha!
Love Michael.

Hi there lovers
All human embryos begin life female. This is the reason men have nipples. So much for Adam and Eve. Black god / White god? = No god. The Creator is ELECTRO MAGNETISM. Time and Space are INFINITE. Have a laugh. "http://www.katebush. com"
Love Michael.

Hi there lovers
The phrase is Creatures of the Universe. Time and space are INFINITE.
Love Michael

Hi there lovers
Time and space are INFINITE and so is Matter. Atoms and electrons are being re cycled. Love Michael.

Does Yoko believe that time and space are infinite? How many shades are there between black and white? How big is the Universe? Love Michael.

Hi there lovers
I do not watch much TV as I believe the powers that be are trying to brain wash me. (1984) Mark Chapman said he could here voices coming from the TV. So who killed John? The organisation who

create the voices or a telepathically hypnotised Mark Chapman? Love Michael.

Imagine the end of money - No need for an auction - Everyone fed and housed. Love thy neighbour Michael

How many atheists have been killed by the christians?
Love Michael.

Hi everyone
I am convinced if we go vegan it will stop all killing of animals including the one we call human beings and we will have peace. We hate vegetables at the moment but deep down we don't really want to kill them either. Actions speak louder than words. You kill and eat vegetables. You hate them at the moment. That makes sense doesn't it. Water House? By the way milk is for cows. Human milk is for humans and don't they do well on fluids! Love thy neighbour Michael

Hi there lovers
Build on agreements rather than differences.
Lover Michael

I love George. I love Osama. In the end the love you take is equal to the make. If I said to Osama and George I love you would they have any reason to hate me? We need to have a referendum on money. I suggest we abolish it. We have laws and choices. Should we make it law to go vegan and extend Thou shalt not kill to animals? Love Michael

War is wrong. While I am not a christian I do believe in Thou shalt not kill hence I am a Vegan (Eat no animal products). I bet you if we all went

Vegan we would not go to war. No matter what George does the only way to get George to love me is for me to Love George and Osama no matter what they have done. The slate needs to be wiped clean. We need to have a referendum on Money and those who control it (telepathic freemasons -I Love them. Cruel Oath destroys all the good they are trying to do. Hence we are at war). I suggest we remove the instrument of Human Greed - Money. Now let us have a vote on Money and masons. Poverty will be made history and we will all be happier. Love Michael

Money is the root of all evil. How do we get rid of evil? Get rid of money. Suggestion MAKEPOVERTYHISTORY ABOLISH MONEY. What would Yoko suggest? Love Michael.

Hi there lovers
If you want a laugh log into "http://www.katebush.com" All you can hear is a bird singing. It makes me laugh. If you do not laugh it may be that the master of the lodge is holding a knife to your throat. You know what I mean. It is wrong. How they can get away with threatening to kill people I do not know. End freemasonry. They appear to control money. The root of all evil. 20000 dying every day through starvation because countries do not want to pay for the food. ABOLISH MONEY. Would John agree? Love Michael.

Hi there lovers
Well done to Yoko for the advert in the Sunday Times in the UK. "Imagine all the people living life in peace". It is about time we came together as one family. Not millions. I believe that the Creator is ELECTRO MAGNETISM. Not a list of gods as long as your arm. All created by the telepathic

freemasons running a dream TV studio in the masons minds. Talk about brain washing. We are not fooled. Black god / White god = No god. Love Michael.

Not while politicians are receiving commission. Love thy neighbour Michael

I would ask the Doctors in the US to detain George under the mental health acts in the US. Love, Truth and Relief. Think it. Say it. Do it. Stop listening to black, brown, white and yellow delusions who are just cartoon characters made up by the lodge to control George and Osama. The lodges are becoming wilder and wilder and appear to be completely insane. Detain the lot of them under the mental health acts in the US and around the globe. I have had enough of their death threats, secrets and lack of relief. The death threats are illegal however I have never rated prison as a way to treat people who have broken the law. Hospital is the place for these people whom we love and want to see them get better as soon as possible. The lodge is at the nucleus of all our global problems and that my friends is the truth. Who controls money in the US? What would happen to the weapons companies if we had peace. What would happen to the stock market in the US if the weapons companies went bust? Peace is bad for business. We need to have a global vote on money. It needs to be abolished so we can sort out the environment, famine and war. How many more will die because we continue to keep capitalism which is at the heart of all our problems and threatens to send our beautiful planet into hibernation? Love thy neighbour Michael

Hi there lovers
Is the truth that John Lennon was a communist
and the powers that be hypnotised Mark Chapman
into killing John? JFK and all that again. What do
you think? Love Truth and Relief should result in
communism and yet we keep ending up with death
destruction and greed. Our friends down the lodge
do not appear to be working. Their oath shows you
why it is not working. Death threats and tongue
cutting are not Love Truth and Relief. Love Michael.

Hi there lovers
Well done to Yoko for the advert in the Sunday
Times in the UK. "Imagine all the people living
life in peace". Imagine no need for greed and
hunger. If we Abolish Money everyone will be fed
and housed. We need a true democracy. Basic to
begin with. See suggestions from anyone on TV
or listen on radio. Then vote using telephone. Dial
1 to feed everyone. Dial 2 not to feed everyone.
No one could argue with the result as this is a
true democracy. Not fascism sponsored by big
business. Are Paul and Yoko friends now? I hope
so.
Love Michael.

Hi Kris
It must be difficult to live in a country which is
at war and no one except the President want
it. Suggest you start a petition and hand it to
George. Better still a phone in vote. I am starting
an interactive democracy called VotePOINT. Our
politicians are taking bribes (donations and loans).
It appears we have to have wars to keep the
weapons companies in business? Love Michael.

Hi there lovers
Remember Time and Space are INFINITE.

The two parallel lines will never meet.
Love
Michael

Hatred comes from within. If you hate yourself
you will hate other people. You will have the gift
of hate. The masons install a hatred program in
people's brains. They then have the gift of hate
and threaten to kill each other by disembowelment
or having the heart cut out. Show you care - Go
VEGAN. Actions speak louder than words. Love
Michael.

Love human beings. Hate rice and eat it. Love
Michael.

Are you saying the US government worked with
the Freemasons to hypnotise Mark Chapman into
killing John Lennon? Love Michael

Hi there lovers
I may come back as a potato.
Love Michael

Would it not be better to simply acknowledge the
Sun and electro magnetism as the creator and
stop messing around with various imaginary gods,
black, white, brown and yellow depending upon
which lodge people go to. We should love thy
neighbour everyday not just on Jesus' birthday and
it was the worst thing ever done to kill him. Mary
was not a virgin. This is a crazy joke. We need to
get real and stop the lodge and church from brain
washing us. Most of us in the western world do not
need any presents while other people have nothing
and are cold and hungry with no sanitation. It is
a sick world we live in. What would Jesus do - a

bottle of perfume or a bowl of rice for someone who is starving? Love thy neighbour Michael

I suggest we all say "I LOVE YOU" to everyone we meet and finish all our correspondence "LOVE THY NEIGHBOUR" as taught by Moses and Jesus. Love thy neighbour Michael
SUN DAY

People who go to mind reader lodges (Most do not work with stone) agree a suicide pact so it is hardly any wonder it is rubbing off on the children. It is illegal. How do they get away with it? Are you hearing my thoughts George and Tony? Time for some Love Truth and Relief and get rid of the secrets, death threats and crazy rituals which contradict Love Truth and Relief. Love thy neighbour Michael

I was interested by Yoko's view on the Universe being approximately infinite. I have spent many hours discussing Time and Space being Infinite. You cannot make or destroy matter according to Einstein. This point of view causes many problems with religion and secret societies who believe in a god and a beginning. Einstein effectively confirmed that all matter has been around forever. Therefore no gods. Black white or any shade in between and NO BEGINNING. I believe Einstein's brain was telepathically attacked by people who felt threatened by the intelligence of Einstein. His brain was remotely attacked by an electro magnetic surge from people who wanted to damage Einstein and "Teach him a lesson". He went down with schizophrenia. I too am schizophrenic and have similar views to Einstein. The church has some good stuff to teach but killing Jesus and celebrating it every year is wrong

and illegal. Moses said Thou shalt not kill. This is
the cornerstone of christianity. So why celebrate
killing Jesus? Good Friday? Sad Friday surely.
Killing a man who was teaching LOVE. Wrong and
illegal but then the masters of the lodge threaten
to kill people every day. Lodges were built in
church grounds while churches were being built by
masons. Most people who say they are masons are
not telling the truth. Most have no idea how to lay
bricks and do not work with stone. Give yourself a
proper name. I suggest telepathicpartnership.com
Modern and a true description of what is going on
between every Hydro Carbons (Living creatures).
It is WRONG and ILLEGAL for the master of the
lodge to threaten people. If you talk Love Truth
and Relief then WALK Love Truth and Relief. Do
not threaten to kill people. Most have not even
got their name down on the Organ Donation list.
No one dies for anyone else. I have never known
anyone shoot themselves through the brain so
their heart could be given to someone in need of
a heart transplant. People are murdered - Just
like Jesus - MURDERED. I suggest get the crosses
down and get hearts up. Let the LOVING begin.
Love Michael.

F is for Fun
Shame George wants to keep making light bulbs.
Did you know it is actually harder to make a light
bulb fail than it is to make one that does not?
Never mind the landfill sites will soon be full of
products designed to fail to keep people working
and not having fun. Imagine a 20 hour week
and playing golf in the afternoons and letting
machines do the work. Plenty of machines have
been invented but stifled to you guessed it To
keep people working. Sad stupid world and life
could be FUN for everyone but George wants
everyone to suffer and die just like Jesus. Hold on

a minute Jesus was murdered. Exactly. George has probably been to church or down the lodge. We want change. We want a better life for everyone. Love thy neighbour and Thou shalt not kill - Love, Truth and Relief and Electro Magnetism. Keep the good bits - Get rid of the nonsense contradictions. Talk the Talk - Walk the Walk. FANTASTIC. Love Michael.

Time and space are infinite. Everything including us is made of atoms and electrons and is recycled forever. No beginning. Matter has always been. Einstein said You cannot make or destroy matter. TRUTH.
Love thy neighbour. Thou shalt not kill. Love .
Truth. Relief. Electro Magnetism is the creator and the destroyer.
Love Michael

We must stop burning fossil fuels as we are killing our planet. What was ice is now changing to water. To do nothing is suicide and murder at the same time. Time for action. Roll on the water powered car and generator and TEGs (Thermal Electric Generators). We do not need to burn fossil fuels. The only reason is the funding mechanism for our politicians who should all be made redundant for cocking up the environment as they are in the pockets of the oil industry. Love thy neighbour Michael

It is a shame people do not love Jesus. Instead they celebrate killing Jesus and think it was a good idea to kill him. Love one another. One family. Not millions of them competing with each other. Love Michael.

Are the various gods illusions? Who created them? Why? Love thy neighbour Michael

The crowd deserves to know the truth. Fighting over various god illusions is causing problems throughout the world when the simple answer is the Sun or more technically electro magnetism. Look around you. Everything is connected to the Sun. This keyboard is made of plastic which is made of oil which comes from fossil fuels which come from trees which needed the Sun to grow. I suggest we stop loving false god illusions and start loving each other. The alternative is nuclear war when we run out of oil. Love thy neighbour Michael

The truth is the SUN. Love thy neighbour Michael

Love thy neighbour Michael

Hi there lovers
Talking about CDs I know it is a bit off to discuss other artists. Have a listen to the new Kate Bush album called Aerial. In fact if you go on "http://www.katebush.com" all you can hear is a bird singing. It makes me laugh so much it is as if there is a subliminal message. There is. I am semi conscious of telepathy. John Lennon would have been interested. I believe that Kate and Paul McCartney are friends of Pink Floyd artist David Gilmour. Well done to Yoko for the advert in the Sunday Times in the UK. "Imagine all the people living life in peace". Fantastic! Love Michael.

Hi there lovers
Well done to Yoko for the advert in the Sunday Times in the UK. "Imagine all the people living life in peace". Abolish Money and the dream will become real. Everyone fed and housed. We need

a proper democracy. Not a fascist dictatorship sponsored by big business. Have a laugh log on to "http://www.katebush.com" . Love Michael.

On the 25th of December we should be feeding the hungry and housing the homeless - This must surely be the wish of Jesus not another senseless gift to people who have everything they need. Peace will follow. Love thy neighbour Michael

Hi there lovers
How are we going to achieve Peace?
1. Abolish money.
2. Go vegetarian or better still vegan.
(Why do we have an Appendix in our body? - Because at some stage in our evolution we lived on high quantities of vegetable matter -The Appendix removes the "green" out of the vegetable matter - Therefore we are naturally vegetarians)
Love Michael

Hi everyone
Milk is for cows.
Love thy neighbour.
Michael

Hi there lovers
Talking about humans as atoms and electrons I made contact with Paul McCartney using telepathy. I had a tingling sensation around my head and heard myself inside my brain asking Paul if he was telepathic while he was being interviewed on BBC Radio 2 in the UK. Paul answered "yes". I do hope Yoko and Paul can love one another.
Love Michael.

If people get hanged for killing people then the end result is everyone will be hanged. Love thy neighbour Michael

I am worried USA will invade Iran and Russia will get upset causing a nuclear war all because it seems Iran has an oil reserve that someone wants to get their hands on. Some will argue oil is the backbone of capitalism. We could switch to alternative energy but it appears there would be a massive power change and jobs would have to change too. In my mind there is only one way to avoid nuclear war and that is to end capitalism and share the global resources and implement new technology allowing people to work less hours and have more free time. Children will still compete at school for the jobs they want and will get their job choice if they work hard at school. We need to avoid this potential nuclear war. Love thy neighbour Michael

Human beings are made of atoms and electrons. I believe that when I die my electrons are absorbed back into the universe's infinite store of electrons and that those electrons will go on to occupy another body. What would Yoko say about this theory of INFINITE life? Anyone hallucinating a god in their mind is a schizophrenic. It is not real. It never ages. Dinosaurs came millions of years before humans. If the bible was correct then gods should look like dinosaurs. Keep "Thou shalt not kill" and "love" Chuck the rest. Michael.

Hi there lovers
Time and space are INFINITE. Would John agree? I am sorry I upset you. We need to know the truth about why John was killed. Love, Truth, Relief and

Electro Magnetism.
Love Michael

Nothing happy about killing Jesus. Worst thing we have ever done. Love thy neighbour Michael

You cannot make or destroy matter. Therefore there is no beginning and there will be no end. Love thy neighbour Michael

Would Yoko be a capitalist or a lover? You cannot be both. Love Michael.

Exactly it is an illusion and George has spoken to it and it is controlling George. It told George to invade Iraq and look at the mess we are in now. Face up to facts we will run out of oil. It will cause the end of capitalism or a nuclear war. Love thy neighbour Michael

No matter what anyone does we must love one another or we become as bad as the people who are causing wars.
Love Michael

Is Yoko, Faithful, Paul McCartney or Freemason? Those in the telepathic world will understand. Love Michael.

Hi there lovers
We had an interesting programme on Channel 4 TV in the UK called "Religion is the root of all evil?" There is no doubt that "Thou shalt not kill" and "Love thy neighbour" are the back bone of our lives and are fantastic. Various gods black or white, male or female are causing friction. Does anyone else out there believe it was a bad idea to kill Jesus? He loved us and we killed him and celebrate

killing him every year. How do you feel about killing Jesus? If we could only agree that ELECTRO MAGNETISM is the one Creator and live as one as John would have wanted. Love Michael.

We are destroying our beautiful planet. We must stop burning fossil fuels. Our politicians will not do anything. Is it because politicians are funded by the oil companies? Love thy neighbour Michael

Hi there lovers
It was terrible to see our brothers and sister in a desperate situation in New Orleans. If these natural disasters continue to happen in the New Orleans area perhaps we should not live there. It is simply too dangerous.
Love Michael Hall.

Hi there lovers
Did you know that all human embryos begin life FEMALE? This is the reason men have nipples. So much for Adam and Eve then. Religion is dominated by male images when in fact the female image appears to come first. I believe we are all made of atoms and electrons and this is part of the reason god must have very good eye sight or a very powerful microscope! I do not know who made the microscope! Seriously I believe the Creator is ELECTRO-MAGNETISM across the entire UNIVERSE. Time and Space are INFINITE. There are no brick walls out there floating around! Well done to Yoko for the advert in the Sunday Times in the UK "Imagine all the people living life in peace". Love Michael

Infinite Electro Magnetism. Does Yoko believe in a human god? Yesterday we had the Roman Catholics with their white god on Pause for

Thought on the radio. Today we had the Muslims
with their brown god on Pause for Thought on the
radio. Who is to be believed? Love Michael.

Electricity inside of me. Love Michael.

Brown or white? Love Michael

Do we want to be controlled by an illusion that
seeks to manipulate the
world or is it time to live in the real world with the
Sun as our maker?
Love thy neighbour Michael

The fmasons need to come clean and own up
to inventing various gods. What is the fighting
all about? There is no god. There is ELECTRO
MAGNETISM. No long haired creature with a beard
wearing white. Love Michael.

Who is behind the idea of a human god? There
is the problem behind religion causing all the
problems or at least some of them. Love Michael.

god is black? No not really god is white with
a beard and in need of a hair cut ELECTRO
MAGNETISM INFINITY. Love Michael.

christian are supposed to believe in Thou shalt not
kill . So why do they still have the death penalty in
the US? Why did they kill Jesus? A good idea hence
the words good Friday? Nothing good about killing
people. What do you think? Why don't christians
all go VEGAN if they believe in Thou shalt not kill?
Hypocrisy? I believe in building on agreements. It
is difficult when the fmasons and christians renege
on their own principles. It appears through killing

Jesus they think they created a licence to sin and get away with it. Love Michael.

Someone should drawer a cartoon of the cross they used to murder Jesus with the words Did this do any good? or Good idea or Bad idea? Love Michael.

What about the killing of Jesus. A bloody disgrace the Romans should apologise. Love Michael.

The christians killed Jesus and celebrate killing him every year. How sick. Love Michael.

Who invented god? The fmasons. Therefore the fmasons instructed George to start a war. Love Michael

Abortion is murder but that is OK because Jesus is a licence to kill? I don't think so? Someone should apologise for killing Jesus. Love Michael.

Jesus was murdered. He did not die for anyone. Love Michael.

Perception. Thou shalt not kill. Go VEGAN. If we all went VEGAN no one would be killed. Love Michael.

We are robots being controlled by fmasons. I still love the fmasons . If I give them love they are sure to give me love one day unless it has been extracted. Once the fmasons come clean that they are reading and manipulating minds their brains will fill with love. Love Michael.

Is it hypocritical to teach Love thy neighbour and Thou shalt not kill while 20000 are dying of starvation ever day? How can we let this happen day after day after day. Let us have a referendum on money. I suggest we abolish money. We will run out of oil and most economies will collapse then in any case. Love Michael.

Religions based on the idea of a human god or gods is a masonic illusion. FACT. Love Michael.

Killing Jesus was the worst thing we have ever done and achieved nothing. People wearing a cross is a disgraceful reminder of just how evil some people are. Love Michael.

Allah Brown or white Could do with a shave and a hair cut!
Love Michael

What can you say about a group of people who celebrate killing Jesus and wear a cross? Sick? Love Michael.

Would Yoko agree to an Interactive Democracy to replace politicians who believe in going to war? Do political parties take donations from weapons companies? We want peace. Does Yoko plan to do any more advertising in the Press or elsewhere? Would Yoko be interested in joining the MAKEPOVERTYHISTORY - ABOLISH MONEY campaign? It will cost money to do. The end result will be the end of Global Poverty which is part of the reason we have war. The other benefit is we would stop burning oil which is money based and in doing so save the environment for future generations to come. We have the technology. It is stifled by you know who to protect industries who are stuck in the dark ages. I If we all went VEGAN (No animal products eaten) would we create a loving revolution? Love Michael

Would Yoko MAKEPOVERTYHISTORY and ABOLISH MONEY? Is poverty one of the reasons for war? If we want peace we need to ABOLISH MONEY. When we run out of oil will the world economy collapse in any case? So why don't we ABOLISH MONEY now. How does Yoko feel about 20000 people dying of starvation every day? How much longer before something is done. There is lots of talk but it appears no one wants to walk? Love Michael.

Hi there lovers
Well done to Yoko for the advert in the Sunday Times in the UK. "Imagine all the people living life in peace". Does any one else out there believe Time and Space are INFINITE?
I look forward to your replies. Paul McCartney? Love Michael

Hi there lovers
Well done to Yoko for the advert in the Sunday Times in the UK. "Imagine all the people living life in peace". Does any one else know the Freemasons are telepathic and can read peoples minds consciously? Is it about time the masons told the truth? I think I have just done it for them! Paul McCartney? Love Michael

Hi there lovers
Thought for the day: Time and Space are INFINITE.
A god appeared from behind a bush and then spent seven days at a bench making things. What do you think? Joke isn't it? I am on the Brown rice vegan diet and doing well.
Start with almonds x7 for calcium and apricot kernels x3 (anti cancer vitamin B17 CHEW)
Brown rice, Soya liquid with calcium and a banana mixed and heated (Rice cooked night before) for

breakfast and lunch (plus apple for lunch). (Eat all the apple as pips contain vitamin B17 anti cancer) Vegetable curry or vegetable chilli with Brown rice for dinner followed by pineapple chunks and a Soya based ice cream (tastes great). Treat myself to plain chocolate Soya based. (tastes similar to normal chocolate). As a doctor once said to me "Milk is for cows".
Love Michael

Hi Yoko
If we love one another then IMAGINE must come true. No possessions, no need for greed or hunger. Although I believe there is an afterlife as Einstein said you cannot make or destroy matter. I believe the same goes for electrons. I am made of atoms and electrons which are recycled. I believe when my old carcass fails my energy moves to a new one. I never die I am transferred. Eternal life. No beginning. No end. The world is a laboratory. The Sun is the Bunsen Burner - Not a bloke sat on a cloud as we are brainwashed into believing. All things bright and beautiful The Sun made them all. Love thy neighbour. Michael

Does Yoko want to join the MAKEPOVERTYHISTORY - ABOLISH MONEY campaign? Love Michael.

Hi there lovers
Well done to Yoko for the advert in the Sunday Times in the UK. "Imagine all the people living life in peace". Does any one else think that money is the root of all evil? Should we have a referendum to Abolish Money? Paul McCartney?
Love Michael

Why is Yoko being pulled into the world of money? John would want us to end money. Love thy neighbour Michael

Ban the cross (it was used to kill a person). Erect hearts (symbol of love). Love thy neighbour. Michael

With all the money involved with the arms industry they do not want peace it is bad for business. We need a vote on money now. VotePOINT interactive democracy. Love thy neighbour Michael

Hi there lovers
Human beings struggle to come to terms with infinity.
Time and space are both infinite. There are no walls out there in space.
Love Michael

The word god is immediately racist under our brainwashed way of thinking. We think human god. You then ask yourself Black or White. Man or Woman. Forget the Freemasons they have created images in our minds. The Creator and Destroyer is Electro Magnetism. It can be good and bad. Hence the word god which derives from the word good is inaccurate. Love Michael

Hi there lovers
Human beings are hydro carbons. We are mainly water and carbon. Our atoms are re cycled. Plants produce oxygen by splitting water into hydrogen and oxygen using sunlight. Humans then breathe in the oxygen and breathe out carbon dioxide. Plants then take in the carbon dioxide and bond it with the hydrogen to create carbohydrates. Humans then eat vegetation and then breath out

carbon dioxide. Effectively atoms and electrons are in a constant state of re cycling. A kind of dynamic equilibrium. Humans are doing there best to upset the equilibrium by burning too many fossil fuels. Eventually the plants and trees will not be able to cope according to the New Scientist magazine. Vegetation will drop considerably over the next 70 years. Then we will be in trouble. We must take action now to stop burning fossil fuels. Water Engine rumours? Solar? Wind? We have the answers. Business sponsored politicians are stifling progress. Who sponsored George Bush? Is it any wonder we are not making changes. George owes the oil industry a favour. Do you agree? Love Michael

Hi there lovers
We are made of atoms and electrons. Einstein said you can not make or destroy matter. It has always been there. It is re cycled. Time and Space are INFINITE and so is Matter. Think about it. Love Michael

Could we have a red heart on the top of the Imagine Peace Tower? Love thy neighbour Michael

The Sun shines every day. It is the clouds that cause the Sun not to be seen. Love thy neighbour Michael

Hi Yoko
I am confused about the Christians. Do you believe John would have thought it a good idea to kill Jesus?

Have you read the Da Vinci Code? Apparently the Christians killed 6 million women because they believed in a female god. I believe the Creator is

Electro-Magnetism and not a man or a woman. Not black or white. Not hairy or smooth skin. Dinosaurs came millions of years before humans and yet people still believe in Adam and Eve? Love Michael

Hi there lovers
Re: John Lennon. I would like to know who hypnotised Mark Chapman? Mark Chapman confirmed he was hearing voices. Is the person or organisation who hypnotised Mark Chapman the real killer? Should they be locked up or sent to hospital? If you read John Lennon's biography, John, according to the book felt sorry for assassins because he too believed assassins were being hypnotised and were not the real killer. So who or what is the real killer?
Love Michael.

Hi there lovers
The real killer is the person or group who hypnotised Mark Chapman with subliminal Big Brother messages sent to Mark Chapman's brain (computer) telepathically via the television. Big Brother is the problem not Mark Chapman. John's biography confirms John felt sorry for assassins. We should all love one another whatever anyone has done. Start by loving yourself. Do not join the freemasons it creates internal hatred leaving you with the gift of hate. Love yourself and you have the gift of love. Agree to be killed by the freemasons and you have the gift of hate. When I sin and I will I expect to go to prison or hospital NOT joining the freemasons. I have asked the freemasons to join me at "http://www.telepathicpartnership.com". They do not want to know even though they know I love the freemasons. Love Michael.

HI there lovers
It is a bit out of order to discuss other artists.
Kate Bush has a new CD called Aerial. Log on to
"http://www.katebush.com" All you can hear is a
bird singing. It makes me laugh. Does it do the
same for you? Telepathy! Music contains subliminal
messages! John Lennon would be interested. # 9
Dream. Love Michael.

Hi there lovers
Yoko may be interested in the latest Kate Bush CD
called Aerial. Log on to "http://www.katebush.com"
All you can hear is a bird singing. It makes
me laugh. Telepathy! Subliminal messages in
the music. Everyone is a brother except Paul
McCartneys and the faithful. Not many of us
left. Using the font Times Roman indicates
freemasonry. Using Arial indicates faithful. What
do you use? R.E.M have an album that has two
alternative CD covers. One Times Roman. One
Arial. Some of their music also makes me laugh
when no one else is laughing. Paul McCartney
also has some material that makes me laugh. Is it
about time the masons stopped threatening to kill
everyone and bring us all together as one family?
"Imagine". Love Michael

Hi there lovers
Well done to Yoko for the advert in the Sunday
Times in the UK. "Imagine all the people
living life in peace". Have a laugh log onto
"http://www.katebush.com".
Love Michael.

Hi Gina
I believe in everlasting life. We have electronic
energy inside us. We are made of atoms and
electrons. When the old body fails for whatever

reason I believe our energy then occupies a new
body. I hope this gives you strength. Thinking
of you. Maybe it is simply too dangerous for our
family to live in risk areas throughout the world.
We see terrible poverty in Africa and ask ourselves
why? I suggest we ABOLISH money and put an
end to greed and hunger. We should live in safe
areas where the soil can support the population.
Each one of us to have a contract to work for
the benefit of our planet linked to an Interactive
Democracy. Not communism without democracy.
Not capitalism with politicians sponsored by big
business who seek to influence government policy.
We will be motivated by the love for one another.
We need to stop burning fossil fuels which appear
to be damaging our environment. The question is
are disasters natural or is the human population
helping to cause them? Love Michael.

Hi Gina
Just trying to save human life. Is it sane to live
somewhere where there are known risks? If we
recognised areas of risk then we could reduce the
number of people killed due to natural disasters.
We live in the Universe. Surely we should live
as safely as we can if we truly love one another.
There are many beautiful places on the planet.
One life lost is too many. I hope you feel the same
way. Love Michael.

Hi there lovers
Maybe we need to live away from
coasts. Check out a concept home I
have come up with. What do you think?
"http://www.waterhousesolarhomes.co.uk" If it
takes off all profits will go to charity unless my
dream comes true the abolition of money. Imagine
no need for greed or hunger. Our dream could
come true. Love Michael.

They probably could not work out what colour their prophet is. Say brown and you upset all the white, black and yellow people and so on. The fmasons have brainwashed everyone. We love the fmasons they hate the faithful. Why? Because they hate themselves. What about the 20000 who will die of starvation today. But then there is no problem. Remember we are all forgiven thanks to the killing of Jesus. And 20000 will die tomorrow and guess what we will all be forgiven. Their god is not very caring or at least the people behind their god. We love the fmasons. If they truly believe in LOVE TRUTH and RELIEF let us abolish money and feed the world. The fmasons need to walk the walk. I believe they are about to change. I HOPE. Love Michael.

Hi there lovers
Humans are atoms and electrons. I made contact with Paul McCartney using telepathy. I do hope Yoko and Paul can love one another. Love is not physical. We love our mothers and fathers. We do not have sex with them! Love and sex have nothing to do with one another. John would want us to all love one another. If two people agree to have sex then why not if they have both reached puberty. Who are we to tell people they can't have sex because they are under 16.
Life should be full of choices and yes we do need laws or we would end up with anarchy. If you can pick up a phone and vote by dialling then you should be allowed to take part in an interactive democracy. Love Michael

Hi there lovers
If two people want to have sex let them get on with it. We should all live as one family.
Love Michael Hall.

Hi there lovers
Variety is the spice of life. Who wants to be owned? If you love someone you set them free. Should we deny Paul some fun. Remember one family. Love Michael.

Hi there lovers
As long as everyone is having fun -No problem. Remember "Imagine" No possessions - Sharing all the world. Live together as one - One family. Love Michael.

Hi there lovers
The phrase of the day is INFINITE RE-CYCLING. I look forward to your comments.
Love Michael

Hi lovers
VotePOINT is our Interactive Democracy
1. Should we ban the cross which was used to kill a man and replace it with a heart which is recognised to represent love?
Love thy neighbour
Michael

Chapter 3

MediPOINT v In Touch With Health

Background

1. MEDIPOINT LIMITED was formed in 1995 to sell computer touch screen systems to Pharmacies / Health sites.

2. MEDIPOINT LIMITED' s other activity included selling advertising space to Pharmaceutical companies for drug adverts to appear on the touch screen program.

3. Patients touch on a computer screen that then qualifies what is wrong with the patient by bringing up a series of "pages" on the touch screen. The system then offers the patient health care advice and a list of drugs to cure the patient's problem.

4. MEDIPOINT LIMITED contracted Visual response Limited of London to provide a computer touch screen health program.

5. MEDIPOINT LIMITED contracted Alphameric of Guildford to install computer hardware, touch screens and satellite installations.

6. MEDIPOINT LIMITED obtained a Consumer Credit License (CCL) and contracted **Nat West**

trading as Lombard to finance MediPOINT installations.

7. National Pharmaceutical Association (NPA)(Trade body representing pharmacists in UK) promoted the MEDIPOINT LIMITED system to pharmacies.

Visual response Limited

8.

a) Visual response Limited did not own the copyright in the text contained in the program they supplied to MEDIPOINT LIMITED and were therefore not entitled to license fees for the program.

b) Visual response Limited did not deliver artwork for customisation of programs to Alphameric for programming despite £800.00 being paid for C G Murray pharmacies systems and were therefore not entitled to money for customisations.

c) Visual response Limited mismanaged the project after Michael Hall had signed an acceptance note in December 1995 by not warning MEDIPOINT LIMITED of the regular requirement for Planning Permission related to satellite dish installations and therefore Visual response were not entitled to management fees of £1000.00 per month.

d) Visual response Limited attempted to sell advertising space to Lisa Elbeck at Windsor Healthcare while still working for MEDIPOINT LIMITED when it was MEDIPOINT LIMITED's role to sell space.

e) Visual response Limited did not process advertisement artwork relating to a product called Tagamet from SmithKline Beecham (Now GlaxoSmithKline or GSK). Without production and programming of artwork featuring drugs we could not charge pharmaceutical companies and therefore our income stream was cut off.

f) Visual response Limited was entitled to money for plastic bags and pens with the MediPOINT logo used at the launch of MEDIPOINT but not for the cost of the exhibition, which was paid by MEDIPOINT LIMITED.

9. MEDIPOINT LIMITED and Visual response Limited had an agreement in place that prevented either party from working on a competing project contained in a "Heads of Agreement" document. It can now be proven that Visual response Limited did breach the agreement by working on a competing project from Siemens, Fujitsu, Brann Limited, British Telecom PLC (BT), Lombard and the Labour Party called "In Touch with Health."

10. Michael Hall gave a design for a computer program including a unique feature called a "Generic skin module" to Visual response Limited that has since appeared in a magazine article in GP Practice and Money on "In Touch with Health."

11. During a court case in April 1997 at the Royal Courts of Justice, Strand, London, Judge Rattee's first words were:

12. **" I suppose the conspiracy theory is out then."**

13. However the featuring of the "Generic skin module" on In Touch With Health is one of the reasons the conspiracy theory is in.

14. Why was Judge Rattee even considering the conspiracy theory?

15. Dawkes Chemist confirmed the Visual response program was not fit for the purpose for which it was sold.

16. David Heffer launched a counter claim while under oath in a separate affidavit saying that the problem with Dawkes Chemist system was due to a faulty touch screen monitor.

17. MEDIPOINT LIMITED has no record of a complaint about a faulty touch screen monitor from Dawkes Chemist in the letter confirming that the product supplied by MEDIPOINT LIMITED was not fit for the purpose.

18. At the Court case in April 1997 at the Royal Courts of Justice, Strand, London Jonathan De Rohan a barrister represented MEDIPOINT LIMITED.

19. At least five pharmacists had confirmed on a letter sent to them and accordingly returned to MEDIPOINT LIMITED that the Visual response Limited program was not fit for the purpose.

20. Jonathan De Rohan chose not to put these letters confirming the Visual response Limited program was not fit for the purpose before the Court.

21. Why did Jonathan De Rohan choose not to put the letters before the Court?

22. Michael Hall will subpoena Jonathan De Rohan.

Alphameric

23. Michael Hall Managing Director and sole shareholder of MEDIPOINT LIMITED signed a confidentiality agreement with Alphameric before setting up MEDIPOINT LIMITED.

24. This document disappeared and could not be brought before the court at the court proceedings in April 1997.

25. Alphameric was slow to install systems.

26. The first two MediPOINT installations for Superdrug used a Siemens computer (Ironically) (Not a normal generic IBM compatible PC as were other installations) containing the Alphameric special computer chips.

27. The first MediPOINT installation for Superdrug in Bristol took six weeks to install and one would maybe expect a delay for "tooling up."

28. The second installation for Superdrug at their Head Office in Croydon was delivered but never installed?

29. However there was then another delay of several weeks to install further systems.

30. This caused immediate financial strain on MEDIPOINT LIMITED.

31. The reason for the delay can probably be explained by the following.

32. It can now be proven that Alphameric were to update an ISDN cable network for Siemens according to a Press Release in Alphameric's offices in Shalford, Guildford.

33. It is now proven that Alphameric were working on the "In Touch with Health" project when Alan Morcombe of Alphameric said:

34. "What am I going to do about British Telecom?"

35. Michael Hall will subpoena Alan Morcombe.

36. The confidentiality agreement was broken and as previously mentioned

had disappeared.

37. Caroline from Alphameric said:

38. "The men are scheming."

39. It is clear now that Alphameric was involved in the conspiracy to damage MEDIPOINT LIMITED.

40. **Alan Morcombe of Alphameric offered Michael Hall, Sole Shareholder of MEDIPOINT LIMITED £1,000,000 for MEDIPOINT LIMITED in 1996 before the court case at Royal Courts of Justice, Strand, London in which the evidence suggests that NPA did lean on a key witness.**

Nat West Trading as Lombard

41. Paul Chapman of Lombard phoned to confirm a conspiracy was taking place involving Lombard.

42. Paul Chapman appeared guilty about what was going on.

43. Paul Chapman was not precise about what was going on.

44. Instead Paul Chapman asked Michael Hall to ask the questions.

45. Paul Chapman of Lombard confirmed Michael Hall's suspicions.

46. Michael Hall will subpoena Paul Chapman.

47. Fujitsu confirmed they could not help MEDIPOINT LIMITED when MEDIPOINT LIMITED approached them at a time when it was clear Visual response and Alphameric had clearly breached a contract and confidentiality agreement respectively with MEDIPOINT LIMITED.

48. Fujitsu confirmed they had a meeting with Lombard.

Fujitsu

49. Fujitsu confirmed they could not help MEDIPOINT LIMITED when MEDIPOINT LIMITED approached them at a time when it was clear Visual response and Alphameric had clearly breached a contract and confidentiality agreement respectively with MEDIPOINT LIMITED.

50. Fujitsu confirmed they had a meeting with Lombard.

51. Michael Hall asked Fujitsu:

52. "Is somebody shaking hands at the top of the tree?"

53. Fujitsu answered "Yes."

Siemens

54. The magazine article on "In Touch With Health" describes the project as a joint initiative between Siemens and Brann Limited.

55. The magazine article on "In Touch with Health" describes the "In Touch With Health" touch screen program as a "Yellow Pages" of information.

56. "Yellow Pages" was a trademark of British Telecom PLC in the period 1995 - 1997.

57. It is clear then that British Telecom PLC was also partnering Siemens, Fujitsu, Brann Limited, Lombard and the Labour Party.

58. "In Touch with Health" is clearly a competitor of MEDIPOINT LIMITED.

59. By the appearance of the "Generic skin module" given by Michael Hall to Visual response Limited it is proven that Siemens / Brann Limited poached the MEDIPOINT LIMITED contractor Visual response Limited.

60. From the Press Release in Alphameric's offices boasting of a contract with Siemens to maintain an ISDN cable network it is proven that Siemens poached the MEDIPOINT LIMITED contractor Alphameric.

Brann Limited

61. Siemens were also in partnership with Brann Limited as mentioned in a magazine article on "In Touch with Health."

British Telecom PLC

62. Yellow Pages a British Telecom trademark was used to describe the "In Touch with Health" touch screen project from Siemens, Fujitsu, Brann Limited, British Telecom PLC, Lombard and the Labour Party.

63. Alan Morcombe of Alphameric said:

64. "What am I going to do about British Telecom?"

65. This question proves British Telecom PLC were a partner in the "In Touch with Health" project.

66. Michael Hall will subpoena Alan Morcombe.

67. British Telecom PLC signed an agreement with the Labour Party to link up Health Care sites using ISDN cables.

68. ISDN cables were mentioned in a magazine article as the system to be used to update the Siemens, Fujitsu, Brann Limited, British Telecom

PLC, Lombard and the Labour Party "In Touch with Health" project.

69. British Telecom PLC were making payments coded "computer expenses" to an illegally set up company called TRIASHA according to the Mail on Sunday and I believe these payments may have been used to sabotage MEDIPOINT LIMITED.

70. TRIASHA was formed by "Terry" of Rothchilds whose name was connected to Garth Gunston whom I worked with at AAH INCA in 1994.

71. Michael Hall will subpoena a British Telecom PLC Officer.

National Pharmaceutical Association (NPA)

72. The evidence suggests NPA did lean on a key witness at Dawkes Chemist to get the key witness to retract a written statement used in a court case at Royal Courts of Justice, Strand, London in April 1997. The written statement from Dawkes Chemist confirmed that the program supplied by Visual response to MEDIPOINT LIMITED and then supplied by MEDIPOINT LIMITED to pharmacists was **"not fit for the purpose for which it was sold." This letter was replaced with a statement that said there was a problem with a faulty computer monitor - This was not the truth.**

Read also Visual response Limited points 15, 16 and 17 in Particulars of Claim document.

73. NPA wrote to MEDIPOINT LIMITED customers inviting them to switch their allegiance from MEDIPOINT LIMITED to Visual response Limited

before the Court case in April 1997.This action
damaged MEDIPOINT LIMITED.

74. NPA wrote a defamatory article in the Chemist
and Druggist magazine sent to MEDIPOINT
LIMITED customers with the headline "NPA severs
relationship with MEDIPOINT."

75. This article appeared before the Court case in
April 1997 and damaged MEDIPOINT LIMITED.

76. Mr Gelleman, a MEDIPOINT LIMITED customer
and a member of NPA said NPA could not do what
they were doing to MEDIPOINT LIMITED.

TRIASHA

77. British Telecom PLC were making payments
coded "computer expenses" to an illegally set up
company called TRIASHA according to the Mail on
Sunday and I believe these payments may have
been used to sabotage MEDIPOINT LIMITED.

78. TRIASHA was formed by "Terry" of Rothchilds
a person whose name was connected to Garth
Gunston whom I worked with at AAH INCA in
1994.

79. What was British Telecom PLC getting for
payments made to TRIASHA?

80. British Telecom PLC would not have been
paying money to TRIASHA without something in
return.

81. Price Waterhouse accountants for British
Telecom PLC recovered the money paid to
TRIASHA by British Telecom PLC.

82. Who else was paying into TRIASHA?

83. Who was receiving payments from TRIASHA?

84. The Front Page article in the Mail on Sunday Financial Supplement claimed the Serious Fraud Office (SFO) was investigating TRIASHA.

85. On contacting the SFO they denied there was an investigation taking place?

Labour Party

86. The Labour Party signed an agreement with British Telecom PLC to link up Health sites using ISDN cables before being elected in 1996.

87. A magazine article on the "In Touch with Health" project mentions their system will be updated using ISDN cables.

88. This points towards the Labour Party being involved in the "In Touch with Health" project.

89. Michael Hall asked Fujitsu:

90. "Is somebody shaking hands at the top of the tree?"

91. Fujitsu answered "Yes."

92. Tony Blair PM moved his family into 10 Downing Street when elected.

93. Tony Blair PM then moved his family out of 10 Downing Street saying that 10 Downing Street was too small.

94. Tony Blair PM then sold his London property and moved his family back into 10 Downing Street which was clearly too small for his family?

95. Michael Hall will subpoena Tony Blair PM to find out what the ISDN cables in Health Sites were to be used for?

The Freemasons

96. Jon Connolly of Warner Lambert a Pharmaceuticals company asked Michael Hall:

97. "Were the Freemasons involved?"

98. Why did Jon ask this question?

99. Michael Hall could not possibly know, as Michael Hall is not a Freemason.

100. Michael Hall will subpoena Jon Connolly.

Other parties involved

101. There may be other parties involved.

102. TRIASHA should be comprehensively investigated to see who else was paying into TRIASHA and who was receiving payments from TRIASHA?

103. According to the article in the Mail on Sunday the Serious Fraud Office (SFO) was investigating TRIASHA.

104. On contacting the SFO they denied an investigation was taking place.

Conclusion

105. This is a complex case in which both MEDIPOINT and Michael Hall were damaged to the point where MEDIPOINT and Michael Hall did not have the money to defend a court case in April 1997 at the Royal Courts of Justice, Strand, London.

106. Justice should be seen to be done.

107. Judge Rattee at the Royal Courts of Justice, Strand, London was right to suspect the conspiracy theory in April 1997.

108. Only now can all the facts be revealed to confirm Judge Rattee was right to consider the conspiracy theory.

109. The evidence now confirms the conspiracy theory to be correct.

110. Any money won will be used to develop and install MediPOINTs.

111. Michael Hall understands that five years on Michael Hall can use the MediPOINT name.

112. MediPOINT intends to install MediPOINT touch screen systems in all homes and Health Care sites.

113. The MediPOINTs could also be used for other applications including an interactive democracy where people vote on issues of the day. We can make the decision on the MediPOINT Touch Screen network to feed and house our population. Every minute a child dies of malnutrition and curable diseases. We cannot allow this to continue.

114. In 1998 Michael Hall was diagnosed with a mental illness and this is partly the reason this claim has taken so long to produce. The pressure of this case could possibly have brought on the mental illness. I confirm I am well enough to complete this document.

Chapter 4

Letters To Tony

Tony Blair
10 Downing Street
LONDON
SW1A 2AA

16 September 0. (Time and space are INFINITE)

Dear Tony

We hope you had a productive meeting at the United Nations. Getting George to think love is like hitting your head against a wall. Is George the person who is stopping you from taking the action needed to rid the world of poverty? It appears Bill Clinton is on side. Sadly I feel the answer is not to raise money because the amount required would cause poverty elsewhere or at least there would have to be a dramatic change in life styles in the G8 countries.
For example-
Change your car every 5 years as opposed to 3 years and send the saved money to the Clinton Hunter trust that would then feed the hungry. Sounds sensible however the car industry would suffer and garages would go bust. You can see the problem can't you. With capitalism there are always going to be winners and losers.

1. I suggest we all get an education where people will compete, but not for money and in doing so will end up with the most desirable career for that individual.

2. For example if a person excels in biology they choose say 5 careers they are interested in. For example:

      1. Doctor
      2. Pharmacist
      3. Nutritionist
      4. Physiotherapist
      5. Dentist

3. The department for careers then allocates the person with a career based on the education success and need for health workers while taking in to consideration the closest to the top of the career choices from the person.

4. The person trains to be- For example a doctor (First Choice).

5. In return for working as a doctor the person receives an autonomous house that produces all its own power, video conferencing/TV display, computer, free use of water powered cars and so on. Simply exchange your services for needed products and services. David on £100,000 a week for kicking a ball? Charles is right the world is out of balance.

6. We have an Interactive Democracy using TV/Radio and telephone to begin with and then switch to Computer Touch Screen.

7. We will have all the **freedom** and **choices** associated with capitalism but all the compassion associated with **love** and no one ever starves to death.

Love Michael Hall

Tony Blair
10 Downing Street
LONDON
SW1A 2AA

17 September 0. (Time and space are INFINITE)

Dear Tony

Ref: **Education**
I studied A level human biology. It appears we evolved from Neanderthal man. There are many ramifications to this knowledge.
Is the pope's god black and hairy as human beings were supposed to have been made in the image of a god? What about the muslim god?

What about adam and eve?
I watched a programme on the BBC, which looked at the human embryo, and the reaction hormones have on the development of the embryo.
It appears all human embryos begin life female and this is why men have nipples. So much for adam and eve.
The **female** image appears to come **first**.

What about dinosaurs? There are many fossils to prove the existence of dinosaurs.

In conclusion do we teach adam and eve and sing "All creatures wise and wonderful the lord god made them all" (Brain washing) or do we teach human biology Neanderthal man and evolution out of water not necessarily beginning on planet Earth? We cannot teach both or we will end up with schizophrenia.
Which is more realistic adam and eve or evolution?
Conflict creates **WAR.**

I received an E-mail stating that gods were invented by the freemasons- This appears to be correct.

Please help us Tony and let us have your opinion on these matters.

1. adam and eve or evolution?
2. The freemasons invented gods and planted the images in people's minds using telepathy- Yes or No?

I look forward to your TV and radio appearance.

Love

Michael Hall

Tony Blair
10 Downing Street
LONDON
SW1A 2AA

30 September 0. (Time and space are INFINITE)

Dear Tony

Ref: Environment

We must stop burning fossil fuels for the sake
of every living species on planet EARTH. If you
cannot make a decision or are worried about being
unpopular then I suggest we have a referendum.

Suggestion from Michael Hall:

Do you agree that we must stop burning fossil fuels
with immediate effect for the love of generations to
come for every species on planet EARTH?

Yes: Planet Earth and every living species are
saved.

No: Every living species will either suffocate,
drown or be burnt to death.

You choose.

We hope people choose the yes answer.

The No answer will be classified as insanity.

Love

Michael Hall

Tony Blair
10 Downing Street
LONDON
SW1A 2AA

Time and space are INFINITE -No we have not
gone mad -You think about it.

Dear Tony

Ref: Ethnic Origin

This is a racist question. Prospect Park Hospital,
Reading, Berkshire and the BBC Volunteer Help
Line 0800 022022 Radio 2 both asked me this
question.

Are we going to be treated differently or the same
based upon our ethnic origin?

The truth according to the Sunday Times is:

70,000 human beings left Africa and populated the
world.

Our Ethnic Origin is Black African - All of us

Bit like god -ha ha. Now there is racism and
sexism. A god most definitely has to be white and
most definitely has to be male. Now where did
those male nipples come from?

I am lead to believe we have to blame the
freemasons for this hallucination. They probably
meant well by trying to create a support
mechanism. However as soon as you say a 'god'
the question is asked what colour and what sex?
Many wars have been fought due to this question

and some are continuing now. I suggest the creator is electro magnetism and it can be good and bad. The creation of living things through the electrical bonding of atoms creating DNA is good. Earthquakes and hurricanes are bad. The word god is incorrect as electro magnetism causes both good and bad to happen so I suggest we stop using the word god, which is based on the word good.

Does this hallucination they call god forgive us for letting 30,000 people starve to death every day? So then forgiveness is killing 30,000 every day when I suggest we feed and house them and give them an education to help them work the land or move them if it is not possible to live there. It is called LOVE.

Love

Michael Hall

Tony Blair
10 Downing Street
LONDON
SW1A 2AA

7 October 0. (Time and space are INFINITE)

Dear Tony

Ref: freemasons and gods

I have had enough of carrying the above
mentioned problems.

**1. It is clear the freemasons are threatening
to kill their members.**

This is illegal.

You are the Prime Minister- You sort the problem
out.

**2. There are no gods. Black, white, yellow or
brown.**

The whole idea was invented by the freemasons.

It is absolute madness to believe in gods.

I do not wish to carry this mad problem.

You are the Prime Minister- You sort the problem
out.

If you are thinking about invading Iran - Don't or
we will end up with a world war.

I know you can hear and see everything I do or say. You probably watched me writing this letter.

It is time for Tony Blair to own the above problems and take action.

Love

Michael Hall

Tony Blair
10 Downing Street
London

18 October 2004

Dear Tony

Ref: <u>Psychological Programming</u>

I eat rice.

I kill the rice by boiling it.

I therefore hate rice.

I have found a major problem with human being mind programming.

People say they love fish and then proceed to eat the fish.

If we ate everything that we loved we would surely end up eating each other, mum and dad and everyone that we love.

The food does not die for anyone it is killed by humans and then eaten by humans.

Therefore we hate everything that we eat.

In the same way Jesus Christ was **murdered**.

<u>Jesus Christ did not die for anyone.</u>

In the same way the Freemasons threaten to **<u>kill</u>** everyone.

The Freemasons do not die for anyone and they should all be arrested for threatening to kill everyone.

Killing yourself does not save another life; it merely kills one person.

I look forward to your response.

Love

Michael

Tony Blair
10 Downing Street
London
SW1A 2AA

14 August 0. (Time and space are INFINITE)

Dear Tony

Hope you had a good holiday. Let me guess Tony you are planning a war on Iran. The next thing we will hear will be that Iran has got nuclear warhead capabilities and that Iran can launch an attack on Britain in 30 minutes. I bet you are going to do nothing about the civil wars going on in Africa. I wonder why? Of course I have got it.

Iran has got that black stuff called oil.

Sudan has got no minerals worrying about.
The next thing we will hear will be that Iran is harbouring terrorists. You see Tony we can see right through. We know how your mind works. Do you not think we should lead by example? If we want countries to disarm then we should take the lead and disarm ourselves and so should America.

The way we lead our lives is killing 30000 people every day.

They are starving and the children do not stop crying. They are desperate. This is cruel beyond any war. Just because people have a different point of view to ours does not necessarily make them wrong. Our capitalist system in the UK and USA is responsible for these deaths every day. Would Jesus approve of the way we lead our lives in the UK and USA? If money were no problem we would pool our resources and make sure every one was fed and housed. Education will lead us to a job and we will have a contract with the planet or maybe the universe to work. It will not be a perfect world. It will be a better one though.

IMAGINE no one starving to death.

Is Paul McCartney any happier with £800 million as opposed to last year when he had £600 million?

Remember the Romans. They killed Jesus.

He did not commit suicide. He did not die trying to save any ones life. Jesus was brutally murdered by the Romans. This brutal act achieved nothing.

There are no prizes for killing Jesus.

Do you think it was a terrible mistake killing Jesus or do you condone this act of violence? The fact that so called Christians celebrate killing Jesus on a cross is sure enough evidence that so called Christians are violent people. The bombs in London were another brutal act of violence.

It appears that one brutal act follows another.

When will the violence stop. I will tell you when it will stop. When so called Christians stop celebrating the brutal death of Jesus and stop wearing that awful crucifix and in fact remove all images of the cross from everywhere. I repeat, there are no prizes for killing Jesus. It will stop when Muslims stop their suicide pacts, which I believe, come from the Freemasons. The Freemasons believe in suicide pacts. Have you read "Inside the brotherhood"? The Freemasons are brainwashing these suicide bombers. There is no heaven with 20 virgins no matter how far you travel up. We have been into space and we have not found any evidence.

We are all made of particles and electrons, which are of INFINITE time.

The creator is infinite electromagnetism.

Not a white, black, yellow or brown man or a woman. Men have got nipples because all embryos begin life female. I also believe that testicles begin life as ovaries and with the introduction of the hormone testosterone (which I believe causes wars) suppresses the growth of breast tissue found in women, grows the penis, turns the ovaries into testicles which then drop into the scrotum. My testicles did not drop and had to be surgically brought down.

Adam and Eve is insanity.

The idea of a human creator is also insanity.

Anyone believing these delusions, because that is what they are, delusions planted in our brains by you guessed it, the Freemasons according to an E Mail I received which I agree with, needs to be detained under the Mental Health Act. You see the Freemasons were asked to explain life but they did not have the benefit of science. Everyone thought Christopher Columbus was mad when he said the world was round but eventually everyone agreed.

It is about time we got a grip on the real truth and stopped the various churches and Freemasons from teaching utter nonsense.

Please Tony do not invade Iran. Keep talking. If you do not disarm nuclear weapons in the UK and USA how do you expect others to disarm. Lead by example. Tell the world that we love people across the world and that we are going to disarm.

Stop burning fossil fuels they are killing our beautiful planet. You do want Leo to be able to breath in 70 years time because if the New Scientist magazine is right we will saturate the planet with carbon dioxide this century even if global warming is not true. Is it worth the risk? The answer is no and you know it. We should all be living in Solar Pods not clay mud huts which is what we have at the moment.

There is more technology in my £4.50 calculator than there is in the £125,000 flat I live in. We have the technology it has been used in space. We know it works. Lets use it before it is too late for all of us.

The only thing stopping you is money. You are probably worried about the effect on oil shares and how that will effect pensions. You are probably worried about the value of existing mud huts and the effect on business collateral tied into properties will be effected by the launching of Solar Pods. Who will want to live in a mud hut when a Solar Pod will provide clean energy with no electricity bill? Ah, but you will not be able to spy on us if 1984 is the truth.

As Paul McCartney sings "In the end the love you take is equal to the love you make."

Love comes from within.

As soon as you agree the masonic oath to kill yourself you immediately hate yourself and lose the gift of love.

The gift of love is replaced with the gift of hate. If you do not love yourself you cannot give the gift of love. The hate gift is then seen in wars, which is what we are seeing in Afghanistan, Iraq and all over the world. The Germans had the gift of hate, which they proved when they killed 6 million Jews. I am not a Freemason and have never consciously agreed the masonic oath.

This is why I would never kill a human being as taught by our mutual friend Jesus who said

1. **"Thou shalt not kill"**

2. **"Love thy neighbour".**

1 and 2 are the most important phrases ever taught so lets abide by them instead of that strange delusion forgiving us and the sin is repeated time after time and we never learn.

Suicide pacts are illegal and the Freemasons should be made illegal immediately.

Love from a worried universal creature.

Michael

Call me on 07762 904079

Tony Blair
10 Downing Street
LONDON
SW1A 2AA

Time and space are INFINITE

Dear Tony

Ref: Iran

It appears the Iranians are in bed with Russia
and China. I suggest we do not invade Iran. If
we do we will have nuclear war. We know this is
all about oil. I suggest we must lead the way and
stop burning fossil fuels. The world could become
unstable when super powers like Russia and China
start choosing sides. Sometimes I get the feeling
certain people want to create instability because it
is beneficial to arms companies.

I suggest you find yourself a piece of A4 paper and
write down what you want for the world. I suggest
you start with:

1. We should all love one another.

Then ask all countries to do the same and write
down their ideas for the world.

**We can then build on agreements rather than
arguing about our differences.**

I met some people recently. One was a muslim,
one was a christian. The interesting thing was the
girl the female person gave birth to is an atheist. If
you think about it this is logical. When confronted
with brown allah god or white christian god she

could not make up her mind and logically came to the conclusion that neither was the truth.

Love

Michael Hall

Tony Blair
10 Downing Street
London
SW1A 2AA

23 September 0. (Time and space are INFINITE)

Dear Tony

Ref: Treat Iraq with love not ramming down walls

War in Iraq is not working.

As Stevie Wonder sings "Just like hate knows that love is the cure".

We suggest the following:

1. Speak to the United Nations.
2. Pull all armies of the world together and create a Global Police Service (GPS).
3. Uniform the GPS in yellow with a large red heart on the front and back of their shirts and jackets.
4. Pull all the tanks out of Iraq and replace with yellow beach buggies or at least open top cars. I.E. Don't look as if you are threatening to kill anyone or be killed by anyone.
5. Allocate everyone with a unique number. Make the interim government redundant and replace with a TV/Radio debate on issues of the day followed by a vote using the telephone. This is a true democracy with no chance of corrupt politicians taking bribes from people who wish to influence government policy. No one can argue with this perpetual referendum system, as it is a true democracy. If you genuinely believe in democracy you will

adopt the system we are suggesting.
If you choose not to adopt the system we will
assume you prefer a dictatorship.

Love

Michael Hall

Tony Blair
10 Downing Street
London
SW1A 2AA

24 September 0. (Time and space are INFINITE)

Dear Tony

Ref: The Aggressor

We have the following questions for the UK.

Who invaded Iraq?

Who is developing nuclear weapons in Aldermaston, Reading UK.

Who developed the AIDS virus (Biological weapon)?

Therefore who is the Aggressor?

Tony, be careful the Russians and Chinese are watching you.

The only way out is to have a referendum on money.

We suggest we abolish money.

If we do not abolish money there will be a world war over OIL.

This will become more likely as we get nearer to running out.

Now is the time to innovate and stop using oil as a fuel, for the love of the children and all generations to come.

All these storms in America, it makes you wonder what is causing them?

Climate change? Burning fossil fuels? Ozone layer? World getting warmer?
Why is this happening? - **<u>MONEY</u>**.

Love

Michael Hall

Tony Blair
10 Downing Street
London
SW1A 2AA

Infinity

Dear Tony

Ref: Iraq 3 Step Plan

1. Change the name of the Iraq Police Force to Global Police Service (GPS).

2. Create an interactive democracy in Iraq by allowing people to vote by telephone, mobile phone or E-mail on issues of the day - No political parties, tribes, politicians or leader. (Suggestion for name -VotePOINT).

3. Ask the masonic lodges to tell the world the truth that the various god images in people's minds were created by masonic lodges and that they are not real - I was taught at school that the **Sun** makes plants and trees grow as many people know by a process called photosynthesis not a man with several cans of green Dulux Weatherseal paint - Anyone singing "all things bright and beautiful" must be regarded as insane.

Love thy neighbour

Michael

Tony Blair
10 Downing Street
London
SW1A 2AA

<Infinity>

Dear Tony

Have you ever thought dinosaurs were around
millions of years before human beings and yet the
Christians and Muslims still believe in a human
god? Why?
The words brain washing come to mind. What do
you think? Free...... If you can guess you agree.
Now you have to decide what to do.

Love

Michael Hal

Tony Blair
10 Downing Street
London
SW1A 2AA

4 April 2005

Dear Tony

I heard with interest that you will be praying for
the Pope in a church.
Praying to which god?
What does your god look like?
Black hair?
Brown hair?
Blond hair?
Blue eyes?
Brown eyes?
Green eyes?
White skin?
Brown skin?
Black skin?
Yellow skin?
A combination of different skin types?
How old?
1 month old?
One thousand years old?
Will you be hoping to meet the dinosaurs when you
die?
What will a dinosaur look like after 65 million
years?
By saying that you are praying you are making
yourself look strange.
Tony you must wake up to reality.

There is no heaven. There is no god.

John Lennon was right with the song imagine. If you continue to persist with this notion that there is a god you will have to be seen by two doctors and a social worker who will detain you under the Mental Health Act.
In your current state of mind you are not well and certainly not well enough to be running the country. I hope you get better soon.

Love

Michael Hall

Tony Blair
10 Downing Street
London
Sw1A 2AA

4 October 2004

Dear Tony

The population is suffering from a delusion called god.

Have you ever thought Black God or White God?

Have you ever thought Penis or Vagina?

Anyone believing in a god rather than Charles Darwin theory on evolution is suffering from a mental illness and should be sectioned under the mental health act.

You simply must make contact with me for a discussion on what to do.

Call me, Michael on 0118 9472346 or on my mobile 07762 904079.

Love

Michael

NB. <u>The UK national anthem is complete madness.</u>

Tony Blair
10 Downing Street
London
SW1A 2AA

11 October 2004

Dear Tony

Ref: The Environment

I have become increasingly worried about the environment.

While listening to the radio I heard a report that confirmed that the atmosphere is becoming saturated with carbon dioxide.

This confirms an article in the New Scientist magazine, which I read some seven years ago, which also suggested the planet would become saturated with carbon dioxide.

Cars, aeroplanes and traditional fossil burning houses are causing a major problem to the environment.

We are faced with a choice either go over to the water engine or some alternative energy or we will all suffocate.

Have you heard of the potato or lemon powered clock?

We could build apartments, which mimic the electro chemical reaction of the potato, or lemon powered clock and create electricity that way.

The effects on the economy of switching over to water or the potato or lemon powered clock theory will be financially disastrous.

Now is the time to abolish money and build apartments, one per person and switch over to the water engine, water generator or the potato or lemon powered clock theory.

If we don't take these measures the world will become impossible to live in.

We will either suffocate or everyone will go bust.

Love

Michael

Chapter 5

Dr Day

Dr Alex Day
Consultant Psychiatrist
Mental Health Services
27 Broad Street
Wokingham
RG40 1AU

<Infinity>

Dear Dr Day

I am due to see you on Monday 23 January at 2PM.

Would you please confirm that you do not believe in:

1. **Adam and Eve.**

2. **Various imaginary gods (Positive symptoms- Hallucinations as detailed in the schizophrenia booklets given to me)**

3. **Christmas (The idea that a mother was a virgin)**

4. **Easter (Killing a man by pinning him to a cross and celebrating it)**

Why Do Men Have Nipples?

These are bizarre beliefs the christians have.

Their suggested diagnosis would be as follows:

1. Schizophrenic

2. E.S.N.

3. Complete idiots.

I look forward to your response.

If you do not confirm I will assume that you are in one of the three categories and suggest you seek help. I ask that you please find me a Psychiatrist who does not believe in the above and cancel my appointment with you.

Love

Michael Hall

Dr Alexandra Day
Consultant Psychiatrist
Wokingham Community Mental Health Services
Wallis House
27 Broad Street
Wokingham
RG40 1AU

<Infinity>

Exhibit one

Dear Dr Day

Please find enclosed a Statement of Truth which will be put forward in Reading County Court. If this fails I will launch a Judicial Review in the High Court. Please sign each individual point in the Statement of Truth if you agree and return to 8 Parsley Close, Lower Earley, Reading, RG6 5GN.

Love

Michael Hall

Dr Alexandra Day
Consultant Psychiatrist
Wokingham Community Mental Health Services
Wallis House
27 Broad Street
Wokingham
RG40 1AU

<Infinity>

Exhibit one

Dear Dr Day

Please find enclosed a Statement of Truth which will be put forward in Reading County Court. If this fails I will launch a Judicial Review in the High Court. Please sign each individual point in the Statement of Truth if you agree and return to 8 Parsley Close, Lower Earley, Reading, RG6 5GN.

Love

Michael Hall

Dr Alexandra Day
Wokingham Community Mental Health Services
Wallis House
27 Broad Street
Wokingham
RG40 1AU

Infinity

Dear Alex

Thank you for your letter. I believe we should keep communicating, as it appears I think differently to others. I need to understand why?

Zoe says she loves fish.
Zoe then proceeds to eat fish. Her choice and not illegal.

I say I love fish.
I do not proceed to eat fish.

So then who truthfully loves fish?

Does Zoe need psychiatric intervention?

You are the expert on the human mind. What do you think?

I look forward to your reply. E-Mail is quicker: telepathic@tiscali.co.uk
I appreciate your time is limited. I am your patient. What is driving me? Is it love or hate? Am I trying to make the world a better place for everyone?

Michael
cc Mary Young
cc Alison Tankard

Dr Alexandra Day
Wokingham Community Mental Health Services
Wallis House
27 Broad Street
Wokingham
RG40 1AU

Infinity

Dear Alex

I play golf with Michael Cachia who also lives in
the Wokingham Area. He is convinced that he talks
to a human god and that when I say something
controversial he tells me that he has to apologise
to this imaginary character. Having recently
watched the film Beautiful Mind with Russell Crowe
playing the part of a Mathematician who became
schizophrenic it appears that Michael Cachia is
experiencing hallucinations similar to our character
in the film. It appears that Michael is not alone.
Tony Blair, George Bush and the Pope all speak of
talking to a god. I am not a doctor however my
diagnosis would be that those people mentioned
are showing schizophrenic symptoms. Maybe being
schizophrenic myself I can spot the signs. "You
need to be one to know one." It is strange that
the character in Beautiful Mind could not add up
that the hallucinations were not getting any older.
It seems peculiar then that Michael, Tony, George
and the Pope have never questioned the fact that
their hallucination of a god never gets any older? It
is also strange that the Terry Wogan show on BBC
Radio 2 on Pause for Thought sometimes has a
Roman Catholic Priest seeming to indicate a white
god and then on the next day they have a Muslim
Preacher indicating a brown god. Has no one
ever thought that the whole idea of gods conflicts

with one another and is therefore a figment of someone's imagination. I had an E-mail from someone who confirmed to me that the various gods were invented by the Freemasons. It would appear that this could be true as the Russell Crowe character nick named one of his hallucinations Big Brother possibly a connection with George Orwell's book 1984 which if you have read it talks of Thought Police. Is it then possible that the Brotherhood - Nick name for the Freemasons are planting the image of a god in people's minds to the point where they believe the hallucination is real when it is obviously not. Mary Young told me that life without a god would be "unimaginable". People who have mental illness do not like to admit to it and cannot see that they are mentally ill. They live in denial. "Virtual insanity is what we are living in" (Song by JK). We have an epidemic on our hands. About time someone told the truth. Suggest you use TV, Radio, Newspapers and other media.

Michael
cc Mary Young
cc Alison Tankard
cc Tony Blair's Doctor

Dr Alexandra Day
Wokingham Community Mental Health Services
Wallis House
27 Broad Street
Wokingham
RG40 1AU

Infinity

Dear Alex

I have just returned from visiting Alison, Charlotte,
Dave and Zoe in Dereham, Norfolk. I notice that
they still say they love their food when it is clear
they cut it up and boil it. I would have thought
if you love something you would not treat it this
way. The truth is that they do not love carrots. The
truth is that they kill carrots proving that they hate
carrots. This goes for all of us who eat carrots.

Ying yang says you cannot love everything.
To survive at this moment in our evolution we
have to murder vegetables and eat them. We
hate vegetables. We have an appendix, which
would proves that human beings can survive as
herbivores as do elephants and horses and many
other animals. I do not know what has made
humans kill and eat animals? It is not natural for
us to eat animals. In fact we maybe poisoning our
bodies with the wrong blood group. You would not
have a blood transfusion with the wrong blood
group blood would you?

My blood test proved good and Dr Chadha
commented that my cholesterol level was very
low and then asked me if I was a vegetarian. I
am a vegan and do not eat any animal products.
I wonder whether people who eat animals and

consume dairy and eggs are going against their natural behaviour and causing their bodies health problems?

The appendix is proof that we can survive as herbivores and many vegans are proof of this. Everything we eat is made of atoms and electrons.

Jesus did not die for any one he was murdered. In the same way vegetables do not die for any one they are murdered.

Have the human population gone mad? Are we brainwashed?

If I could find a psychotherapist would you be prepared to pay? I think in a different way to many other people and I need to understand why?

Love to everyone there.

Michael Hall
cc Alison Tankard

Dr Alexandra Day
Wokingham Community Mental Health Services
Wallis House
27 Broad Street
Wokingham
RG40 1AU

Infinity

Dear Alex

Thank you for your letter. Dr Chadha is happy to refer me to a psychotherapist.

This is a difficult time of the year for me. Images of crosses and chocolate eggs everywhere.

Do you think it was a good idea to kill Jesus?

Will you be celebrating the killing of Jesus?

Why do they call it good Friday?

Should it be called good Friday or bad Friday?

Do you believe the people who celebrate the killing of Jesus are brainwashed?

Do they have a mental illness?

Will you be taking action to treat people who have a mental illness?

Can no one else see how wrong the celebration of a brutal murder is?

Love to everyone there.

Michael Hall
cc Alison Tankard
cc Police - New Scotland Yard
cc BBC
cc Tony Blair

NB. How much longer will you let the freemasons threaten to kill children, women and men or is it a suicide pact? The Police say suicide pacts are **illegal**. Why is nothing happening?

Dr Alexandra Day - Circulate to other doctors
including Sally Cubbin
Wokingham Community Mental Health Services
Wallis House
27 Broad Street
Wokingham
RG40 1AU

Infinity

Dear Alex

Hope you had a good break. I was disappointed
to be put on the psychotherapy waiting list for 8
months. The mind is a complex computer with
many chemical reactions going on. Chemical
reactions are caused by energy just like in a
chemistry laboratory. The human body is made of
atoms and electrons and so is a TV and remote
control. Could it be that where there is a difference
of opinion the mind is subjected to an electro
magnetic force and a chemical reaction takes place
in the brain causing mental illness or as I call it
now electro magnetic interference?

After my last stay in hospital I went on a course
which was quite useful. I now try to build on
agreements with people. I look for the positive
rather than the negative. Now I believe in "Thou
shalt not kill", "Love thy neighbour", "Love, Truth
and Relief" but those who said they also believe in
these ideals do not carry them out. Actions speak
louder than words. The goal posts have been
moved and it appears the christian community
believe it was a good idea to kill Jesus. Hence the
phrase "good Friday". These people are not well.

I believe my problems are ones of a religious nature. The way I think undermines some beliefs held by various religious and lodge (most have never worked with stone in their lives and are therefore not masons) groups. A bit like being the living Da Vinci Code. Let's be honest millions of women were burnt at the stake because their opinion was different to that of the christians hundreds of years ago. Up until only 200 years ago atheists were sentenced to death. What happens to these people today? I bet some go down with electro magnetic interference (mental illness).

Would you please put me in touch with a psychiatrist who believes it was a bad idea to kill Jesus and does not believe in various gods with black, white, brown, yellow or any other combination of skin colour. So when the planet was covered with dinosaurs we had a male white human god with a penis? People who believe this are not well. I do not believe in Adam and Eve. I believe all hydrocarbons were created by electro magnetism and that all hydrocarbon life forms came out of the sea. Find me someone who thinks the same logical way. I am taking Flax Seed Oil twice a day as prescribed by Patrick Holford.
Love thy neighbour.
Love
Michael

Chapter 6

The Police

Chief Inspector
Lower Earley Police Station
Lower Earley
Reading
Berkshire

Infinity

Dear Chief Inspector

I telephoned the police to ask you if it was illegal to threaten someone with no less a penalty than that of having my throat cut across, my tongue torn out by the root ... They are supposed to believe in Love, Truth and Relief. If you love someone you would not threaten them with penalties of death for telling the truth. People should have no secrets or the human becomes insecure.

The people who threaten to do this are based at the Berkshire Masonic Centre, Sindlesham, Reading. Please detain these patients under the Mental Health Act by sectioning them. If they refuse to be detained there will be no other choice than that of arresting these patients, as they are not well. I love them all. They need to be cared for until they can get over their mental problems.

They also believe in gods. These are hallucinations. They never get any older and never change their clothes. Some believe in a brown god. Some believe in a white god. I spoke to a mason who told me there was a choice of gods! So who is right? Neither. It is all made up nonsense. Anyone believing in these hallucinations is not well. Electro magnetism is the Creator and Destroyer. Men have nipples because all human embryos begin life female as is now proven by scientists. So much for Adam and Eve and humans being made in the image of a god. Dinosaurs were around millions of years before humans.

I studied human biology at A level. Do I believe the scientific knowledge taught by my teacher or a book, which is 2000 years old when the world was still flat and people thought they would fall off the edge? The patients are not well.

The Police person who took the telephone call said no crime had been committed. It appears then that the Police person who took the call is also suffering from the metal illness as described above.

I have spoken to Dr Chadha based in Earley and he said about freemasonry and I quote "It is madness". Time for action. Detain the patients.

Michael Hall

Metropolitan Police
New Scotland Yard
London

Infinity

Dear Metropolitan Police

I understand you are investigating the Labour
Party and possible corruption.

The Labour Party signed an agreement with BT to
link up health care sites with ISDN communication
cables in 1996. There were headlines in the
press as the Labour Party was boasting of the
deal they had done with BT. The Conservatives
thought it was a cheek, as the election had not
taken place. BT were making payments totalling
nearly £1 million to an illegal company called
TRIASHA LIMITED according to the Mail on
Sunday. TRIASHA LIMITED had been set up by a
man called Terry of Rothschilds a city investment
company according to the Mail on Sunday. While
working at INCA LIMITED we received a fax from a
Terry of Rothchilds. I cannot remember who it was
addressed to. If you phone me I can tell you who
worked for INCA LIMITED. 0118 9875234 or 07762
904079.

I hope you are successful. From what the media
are saying it appears the political system needs
a complete overhaul. It appears political parties
are taking money in exchange for peerages
or business contracts. I thought politics was
supposed to be impartial?

Michael Hall

Chapter 7

Water House Projects

AUTONOMOUS HOUSE PROJECT

UPDATE 1

To: Prospective Project Members
From: Michael
Water House Solar Homes
Tel: +44 118 9875234
The idea being to design and build an Autonomous House. By autonomous we mean off grid and other usual services. Please read the update below and then confirm if you would like to become a Project Member.
1. PV Solar Panels (Produce 100KWHs per year per square metre) to charge a central battery to produce 1KW to run Ground Heat Pump.
2. Ground Heat Pump will produce hot water to a temperature of 55 degrees c.
3. Hot water to be stored in a Hot Water Cylinder in the base of the Autonomous House.
4. There will be a Thermal Electric Generator (TEG) in the Hot Water Cylinder to produce more electrical energy charging up the central battery in the base of the Autonomous House.
5. We hope to use the "http://www.solardome.co.uk" outer shell which is made of Aluminium and glass in a modular design.
6. The base could be made in Aluminium sections to contain

a) Battery
b) Cold Water Tank
c) Hot Water Cylinder containing Thermal Electric Generator (TEG)
d) Air Conditioning
e) Heater
f) Spa Pool
g) Storage
h) Computer
i) Spare
7. Borehole in a central position to supply water and heat fluid for Ground Heat Pump.
8) The Base Manufacturer will need to know the dimensions of the equipment that will be fitted into the base of the Autonomous House.
Please confirm if you would like to join the Autonomous House Project.
Love thy neighbour
Michael
cc Lennart - "mailto:lennart.holmgren@termo-gen.se" TEG and Battery
cc Bruce - "mailto:bruce@solardome.co.uk" Outer Shell
cc Mike Elgar - "mailto:mike.elgar@taurusenv.co.uk" Waste
cc "mailto:info@iceenergy.co.uk" Ground Heat Pump + Borehole
cc Sally - "mailto:sally@ecoheatpumps.co.uk" Ground Heat Pump
cc Ian Duvall - "mailto:ian.duvall@magal.co.uk" Aluminium Base
cc John Chandler - "mailto:john.chandler@albionwaterheaters.com" Hot Water
cc Steve - "mailto:steve@windandsun.co.uk" PV Solar Panels and Battery
cc Chris - "mailto:enqs@daleswater.co.uk" Borehole

cc Mary Cole - "mailto:mc@bgs.ac.uk" British Geological Survey - Borehole Survey
cc "http://www.shamasbattery.com/en/prosort.asp?mid=5" Battery
cc "mailto:ian.gough@wokingham.gov.uk" - Wokingham DC - Environment

Hi Steve
I will start by saying I am not a capitalist I am an environmentalist. RG Water House has been set up to install Hot Water Cylinders with TEGs into New Build and Existing Houses. They are old fashioned but there are lots of them and we need to be making the best of what we already have. I suggest you contact our TEG developer "mailto: lennart.holmgren@termo-gen.se" to take the idea further. Your Hot Water Cylinders could be creating electricity so why not do it. It makes sense from an environmental point of view. Love thy neighbour Michael

Hi Lennart
I am talking to "mailto:steve.woollas@albionwaterheaters.com" re fitting a TEG into a hot water cylinder. You may wish to make contact. Love thy neighbour Michael

Hi Lennart
Steve Woollas from Albion Water Heaters will be contacting you. The future of the planet is in your hands. The choice is yours. The Sun is a chemical reaction in dynamic equilibrium. We should be using it. We will run out of oil sooner or later and we are not prepared for it. We have the technology so let's use it for the benefit of future generations including people in the current energy businesses and their children or should I say to the benefit of every living thing on the planet. Not much at stake then guys? Love thy neighbour Michael
cc "mailto:steve.woolas@albionwaterheaters.com"

Thank you

Thanks to my teachers at school, scientists in this paper and most of all anyone who has taught me love and made me the person I am today. It is only with their help that I could write this Teaching. Thanks to David the person who taught me honesty is the best policy - Fantastic programming.

Address: 8, Parsley Close, Lower Earley, Reading, UK, Universe RG6 5GN

Telephone: 0118 9875234 or 07762 904079

E-mail: michael@telepathicpartnership.com

Meet the author:
Michael - (Member No.RG0001)
www.rgsinglesclub.org.uk

Religion
www.telepathicpartnership.com

Other initiatives:

Environment
www.rgwaterhouse.co.uk
www.waterhousesolarhomes.co.uk

VotePOINT (Interactive Democracy on Touch Screen) and Information
www.homepointtouchscreensystems.co.uk

About the Author

Vicar Michael is the name I have chosen as it removes my second name or some would say family name. I have done this as I believe we should behave as one global family. I have used the name Vicar as I founded telepathicpartnership. com as an alternative to current religions and secret societies. I was born in the Universe like everyone else and have been living for an infinite amount of time. The particles I am made of have been recycled an infinite number of times and cannot be made or destroyed and are infinitely small. I had an average education which I have found useful. My strength is to bring facts together to create greater strength by associating one science with another. I have received much of the programming that many others have received in my computer brain. I operate my brain in a similar way to a computer by opening and closing folders. I have done many jobs including selling cars and running a touch screen computer company called MediPOINT. When MediPOINT entered into a court case at The Royal Courts of Justice, Strand, London and the Judge said "I suppose the conspiracy theory is out then" and MediPOINT was wound up it drove me to ask the question who is running our legal system? The court case drove me to frustration and I ended up in a mental hospital with the diagnosis of manic depression which has more recently been diagnosed as schizophrenia for which I take medication. So is it mental illness or remote control? Who presses the remote control and why?

Love thy neighbour Michael